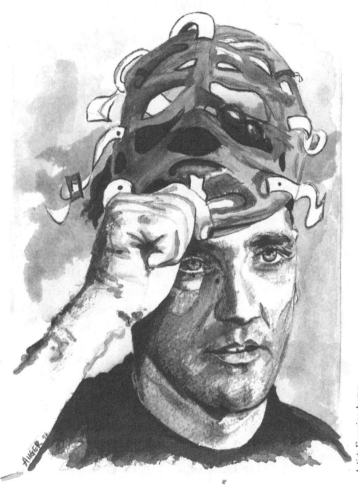

Artist: Francine Auger

Jacques Plante, 1929-1986.

Raymond Plante

Prolific novelist and scriptwriter Raymond Plante has written several television series for young people, produced by Radio-Canada. He was also responsible for two series of novels for adolescents, published by Québec/Amérique and Éditions du Boréal. He has written over twenty-five books, nineteen of which are for young readers. His works have been translated into English, Dutch, Chinese, Greek, Spanish, Catalan, and Basque. He is the recipient of many awards, including the Canada Council Prize for Literature, Youth Category (1986), the 12/17 Brives-Montréal Prize (1994), and the Mr. Christie's Book Award (1995). Recently, he contributed to the hockey nostalgia anthology, *Une enfance bleu-blanc-rouge*, published by Les 400 coups.

The Translator: Darcy Dunton

Darcy Dunton attended the Université de Montréal and McGill, earning degrees in art history and anthropology. Among her translations from French to English are the novel *Cristoforo* by Willie Thomas, (XYZ éditeur, 1997) to be published in 2001 by Breakwater Books, and *The Encyclopedia of Home Winemaking* (XYZ Publishing, 1998).

Editorial correspondence:
Rhonda Bailey, Editorial Director
XYZ Publishing
P.O. Box 250
Lantzville BC
V0R 2H0
E-mail: xyzed@telus.net

In the same collection

Jacques Plante

Canadian Cataloguing in Publication Data

Plante, Raymond, 1947-

[Jacques Plante. English]

Jacques Plante: behind the mask

(The Quest Library ; 11)

Translation of Jacques Plante.

Includes bibliographical references and index.

ISBN 0-9688166-2-2

1. Plante, Jacques, 1929-1986 – Juvenile fiction. 2. Hockey goalkeepers – Quebec (Province) – Biography – Juvenile fiction. I. Dunton, Darcy. II. Title. III Title: Jacques Plante. English. IV. Series: Quest library; 11.

PS8581.L33J3213 2001   jC843'.54   C2001-940383-6
PS9581.L33J3213 2001
PZ7.P52Ja 2001

Legal Deposit: Second quarter 2001
National Library of Canada
Bibliothèque nationale du Québec

XYZ Publishing acknowledges the support of The Quest Library project by the Canadian Studies Program and the Book Publishing Industry Development Program (BPIDP) of the Department of Canadian Heritage. The opinions expressed do not necessarily reflect the views of the Government of Canada.

The publishers further acknowledge the financial support our publishing program receives from The Canada Council for the Arts, the ministère de la Culture et des Communications du Québec, and the Société de développement des entreprises culturelles.

Chronology and photo research: Michèle Vanasse
Index: Lynne Bowen
Layout: Édiscript enr.
Cover design: Zirval Design
Cover illustration: Francine Auger

Printed and bound in Canada

XYZ Publishing
1781 Saint Hubert Street
Montreal, Quebec   H2L 3Z1
Tel: (514) 525-2170
Fax: (514) 525-7537
E-mail: xyzed@mlink.net
Web site: www.xyzedit.com

Distributed by:
General Distribution Services
325 Humber College Boulevard
Toronto, Ontario   M9W 7C3
Tel: (416) 213-1919
Fax: (416) 213-1917
E-mail: cservice@genpub.com

PLANTE

Jacques

THE QUEST LIBRARY

BEHIND THE MASK

XYZ
Publishing

Books by Raymond Plante

Novels for young people:

Monsieur Genou, "Jours de fête" series, Leméac, Montreal, 1981. Awarded the Prix belgo-québécois (1982).

La Machine à Beauté, Jeunesse/Romans series, Éditions Québec/ Amérique, Montreal, 1982. Reprinted in the Boréal Junior series, No.11, Éditions Boréal, Montreal, 1991. Awarded the ACELF prize (1982); translated into Spanish and Catalan.

Le record de Philibert Dupont, Jeunesse/Roman series, Éditions Québec/Amérique, Montreal, 1984. Reprinted in the Boréal Junior series, No.12, Éditions Boréal, Montreal, 1991. Translated into English, Spanish, and Catalan.

Minibus, (short stories), Jeunesse/Romans series, Éditions Québec/ Amérique, Montreal, 1985.

Le dernier des raisins, Jeunesse/Roman series, Éditions Québec/ Amérique, Montreal, 1986. Reprinted in the Boréal Inter series, No.11, Éditions Boréal, Montreal, 1991. Awarded the Canada Council prize for literature, youth category (1986). Translated into English, Dutch, Spanish, Catalan, and Basque.

Des hot-dogs sous le soleil, Jeunesse/Roman Plus series, Éditions Québec/Amérique, Montreal, 1987. Reprinted in the Boréal Inter series, No.12, Éditions Boréal, Montreal, 1991. Translated into *Spanish and Catalan.*

Y-a-t-il un raisin dans cet avion? Jeunesse/Roman Plus series, Éditions Québec/Amérique, Montreal, 1988. Reprinted in the Boréal Inter series, No.13, Éditions Boréal, Montreal, 1991.

Le raisin devient banane, Boréal Inter series, No.1, Éditions Boréal, Montreal, 1989.

Le roi de rien, Roman jeunesse series, La Courte Échelle, Montreal, 1988. Awarded the ACELF prize (1988). Translated into Spanish, Chinese, and Greek.

Véloville, Premier Roman series, La Courte Échelle, Montreal, 1989. Translated into Spanish.

Le chien saucisse et les voleurs de diamants, co-authored with André Melançon, Boréal Junior series, No. 9, Éditions Boréal, Montreal, 1991. Translated into Catalan.

Les dents de la poule, Boréal Junior series, No. 22, Éditions Boréal, Montreal, 1992. Awarded the Monique Corriveau prize (1993).

La fille en cuir, Boréal Inter series, No. 24, Éditions Boréal, Montreal, 1993.

L'étoile a pleuré rouge, Boréal Inter series, No. 28, Éditions Boréal, Montreal, 1994. Awarded the Prix 12-17 Brive/Montréal prize (1994) and the Mr. Christie's Book Award, 12 and over category (1995).

Un monsieur nommé Piquet qui adora les animaux, La Courte Échelle, Montreal, 1996.

Les manigances de Marilou Polaire, La Courte Échelle, Montreal, 1996.

Véloville, La Courte Échelle, Montreal, 1997.

Le grand rôle de Marilou Polaire, La Courte Échelle, Montreal, 1997.

Le long nez de Marilou Polaire, La Courte Échelle, Montreal, 1998.

Élisa de noir et de feu, La Courte Échelle, Montreal, 1998.

Attention, les murs ont des oreilles, La Courte Échelle, Montreal, 1998.

Marilou Polaire et l'iguane des neiges, La Courte Échelle, Montreal, 1998.

Novels for adults:

La débarque, L'Actuelle, Montreal, 1974. Awarded the L'Actuelle prize (1974).

Le train sauvage, Littérature d'Amérique series, Éditions Québec/Amérique, Montreal, 1984.

Avec l'été, Éditions Boréal, Montreal, 1991.

Un singe m'a parlé de toi, Éditions Boréal, Montreal, 1993.

Projections privées, La Courte Échelle, Montreal, 1997.

Contributed to the hockey nostalgia anthology, *Une Enfance bleu-blanc-rouge* (Les 400 Coups, Montreal, 2000), with "La Société des partisans disparus."

Acknowledgments

I would like to thank Ms. Renée Gravel, who accomplished a prodigious research job, compiling a huge number of newspaper and magazine articles that were written during Jacques Plante's career. I would like to express my appreciation to the employees of the microfilm room of the Bibliothèque nationale du Québec, in Montreal, for their kindness, competence, and zeal in assisting Ms. Gravel in her task, as well as the employees of the National Archives in Ottawa. Finally, I would like to thank Ms. Andrée Poulin, journalist, and Ms. Claire Couture, producer at Radio-Canada in Ottawa, both of whom gave me some interesting leads, and Mr. Boguslav Podorsky of the archives at Radio-Canada, who allowed me to consult audio-visual documents.

Contents

First Period

From Shawinigan
to Chicago

In 1944, Jacques Plante plays in four different categories:
midget, juvenile, junior, and intermediate.

1

A Taxi in Chicago

Saturday, April 4, 1953.

This time, it was for real. Jacques' hands were shaking. His skate laces had never given him so much trouble – they had never been so stiff. Nor had the straps of his leg pads ever seemed so numerous and so difficult to buckle.

His hands were trembling so hard that he wondered if he would be able to use them properly. How could he stop the streaking pucks? Would his wobbly knees even hold him up? Would he be able to move fast enough to block surprise rebounds?

He brushed these thoughts away. If a hockey goaltender wants to overcome the incredible tension that he faces at game time, the last thing he should do is visualize the puck getting past him. Like a fighter shadowboxing before a match, he has to fan the spark that will ignite each one of his movements and give them perfect precision: the lateral slide that will send the puck into the corner of the rink, the block by a leg projected outward with lightning speed, the last-minute dive, and the spring that will bring him up ready, agile as a cat, to stop the faster and even more dangerous shots off a rebound.

The whole game depends on the goalie. He is the last player that the adversary must try to outplay, the one whose smallest mistake is irreparable, fatal – the one who can save the game when he faces an opponent on a breakaway, and the one whose failure demoralizes the whole team. The goaltender is the only player who must never lose sight of the puck, even for a fraction of a second. He has to continually sharpen his concentration in spite of the unbearable heat, the yelling crowd, his fear of injury, scrambles in front of the net, a teammate's error, or the superior power of the opponents. A goalkeeper has to harden his shell: whatever happens, he must be a solid wall, a fortress.

But Jacques Plante was also a man. A solitary man, whose hands were trembling now. In spite of the confidence he had built up over the years, in spite of his talent and his famous reflexes, his hands were still shaking. His knees were almost knocking together. He couldn't let the team down.

This was the game that had to be won – absolutely. The Montreal Canadiens had their backs to the wall, and he, Jacques Plante, owed it to himself to triumph, to show that he was the man of the hour. Tonight, he was living his life's dream.

The dressing room of the old Chicago stadium reeked of sweat and fear, the fear that drives champions to excel, to fight with their last ounce of strength to be able to revel in the taste of victory – and to save their skins. The atmosphere in the dressing room resembled a pumping heart pulsing with electricity.

Maurice Richard, the soul of the Habs, was sitting nearby, and Jacques could see that his hands were trembling too. The Rocket looked over at him. He never talked much, but used his flashing eyes to communicate with his teammates – or to intimidate his opponents during a game. This time, however, he spoke to Jacques in a low voice: "I'm nervous too. Don't worry about it – it's always like this before an important game. It'll go away when you've been on the ice a few minutes."

Tonight was *the* important match of the season. On that springtime Saturday, the Canadiens were facing sudden death. The Black Hawks were leading the best-of-seven semifinal series 3 to 2. One more defeat, and it was all over. A single loss and Jacques Plante would be sent down to the minors, where he would likely disappear and be forgotten.

Jacques was alone, infinitely alone, like all those of that special brand of athletes, goalkeepers. He suffered the same pre-game nervousness as the other players, he wore the same uniform, but he had a completely different job to do. Managers and sportswriters repeated it endlessly: without a strong goalie in the nets, a team had no chance of winning the Stanley

Cup, the ultimate prize for each of the six great teams that made up the National Hockey League – the world championship, in fact. And now, the Habs were counting on him. Jacques' hands weren't shaking for nothing. He had to empty his mind to resist the crushing pressure that could make him slip up badly.

Just a few hours earlier, Dick Irvin Senior, the Canadiens' coach, had knocked on the door of Jacques' room at the Lasalle Hotel.

"You're coming in the taxi with us."

The brief sentence was the equivalent of an order. Jacques, who had travelled with the team as backup goalie, was startled. The white-haired coach was known for his original ideas; he loved to baffle the opponents by his unexpected tactics. Only the opponents? Not necessarily: often, by shuffling the cards, he set challenges for his own players; that was how he pushed them to try harder and play better. But even then, the young goaltender did not realize what was awaiting him.

In the taxi, Irvin sat in the front seat. Jacques slid into the back between Tom Johnson and Doug Harvey, both solid defencemen who were maintaining a tense silence.

The taxi set off, a metal box full of nerves in the light of the lengthening days of spring, amid the wind that was swirling loose pieces of paper all over the Chicago streets, as usual.

After a moment, Dick Irvin turned around, as if he had just reached a decision, and barked, "Jacques, you're replacing Gerry McNeil tonight."

The young man caught his breath. Naturally, with the Canadiens in a tight spot, the Silver Eagle, as the reporters had dubbed Irvin, was entitled to pull a surprise move. But McNeil wasn't injured, and his performance until the playoffs had been impeccable. He had even stopped Gordie Howe from scoring his fiftieth goal in the last game of the regular season. By doing so, the goalie had protected his teammate Maurice Richard's record as the only offensive player to have scored fifty goals in one season.

The fact of the matter was that McNeil himself had asked the coach to replace him. He had become too nervous during the playoffs. In the preceding games, he had fumbled the puck several times, and knew that it had put his teammates off their stride. Before getting out of the taxi, Dick Irvin turned around again, and, as if he wanted to startle his young goaltender out of his daze, said in an authoritative voice, "And you're going to get a shutout tonight."

Not another word: silence, except for the howling Chicago wind. If the old wizard had wanted to cast a spell on Jacques, he could not have done it better. Jacques felt that his heart was about to stop beating. But Johnson and Harvey were already hustling him along the sidewalk. Irvin, the cunning fox, not only wanted him to be good – he wanted him to be perfect! A goaltender must always be perfect. Jacques was shaking all over now. Between the two star defencemen, he felt that he was of little account. When he entered the stadium, he had the impression that he was sleepwalking.

In the dressing room, after all his equipment was laced, buckled, and tightened ready to play, Jacques was feeling shakier than ever. He was barely aware that the coach was making radical changes to the lineup, sending in team members who hadn't played in the series at all so far.

Jacques was in the full throes of goalkeeper's anguish, but at the same time, he recognized the thrill deep within himself that had always spurred him on to give his best. Since he had fallen in love with this sport, he had never bowed to pressure no matter what obstacles had to be overcome, and he had always tried to surpass himself. Jacques always loved to rise to a challenge. He enjoyed playing under pressure and fighting against his own nervousness. He often told himself that true champions are revealed in difficult moments. And Jacques Plante's desire was to be a true champion – nothing less would do.

Until then, things hadn't come easily to him. He had painstakingly climbed each step of a difficult ladder to reach his present situation. At twenty-three, he wasn't a kid anymore. Dick Irvin had finally given him the chance to achieve his most cherished ambition. He would have other, perhaps higher ambitions in the future – he was certain of it.

Jacques got up, feeling his leg guards tight against his legs. He adjusted his chest pad and the last pieces of protective equipment before donning the white sweater emblazoned with the superimposed red and blue "CH" that made all Quebec youngsters dream. He passed his hand over his pounding heart as he pulled the sweater over his diaphragm.

Jacques looked around at the others – at the younger ones, "Boom-Boom" Geoffrion, Dickie "Digger" Moore, and Dollard St. Laurent; then at the veterans, Émile "Butch" Bouchard, Elmer Lach, Bert Olmstead, Billy Reay, and Ken Mosdell. They were his partners – men who were in a cold sweat just like he was, and who all had one thought in their minds: to win.

Again, Jacques turned towards The Rocket, who was still sitting down, his piercing black eyes fixed on an invisible point, as if he were watching the opponents' goalie and planning a manoeuvre to get past him. More than anything, Maurice Richard hated to lose. For a fleeting moment, Jacques had the impression that he was among Titans.

Was he dreaming? Was he, Jacques Plante, the kid from Shawinigan, really standing in the dressing room of the Chicago Stadium with the Montreal Canadiens?

A familiar scene from his adolescence flashed into his mind.

It was spring, 1944. He was fifteen years old. His family did not have enough money to buy a radio, but, luckily, the upstairs neighbours had one, and it was tuned to the nasal, play-by-play commentary of the Stanley Cup playoff games. Through the ceiling of his sisters' room, "le grand Jacques" could hear what was happening on the far-away rink. But that wasn't good enough: he would climb on top of his sisters' bedroom furniture to be closer to the ceiling so that he could hear better. Upright on a chest of drawers, Jacques tended an imaginary net, using his hands and feet to help Bill Durnan, the Canadiens' rookie goalie, stop the killer shots. That was how he "played" with the Habs that year: it was his way of helping his club beat the Chicago Black Hawks to win the 1944 Stanley Cup.

The familar names came down through the ceiling: Maurice Richard, Elmer Lach, Toe Blake, Butch Bouchard – athletes, heroes, gods. In Jacques' excited imagination, every one of the players whose exploits came to him as if from heaven above were at least ten feet high.

Now it was his turn to stand among the gods – in real life.

Of course, it wasn't the first time. During the regular season, when Gerry McNeil had fractured his jaw, Irvin had brought Jacques in for three games. The young man had not disappointed him.

However, there had been the famous tuque affair – the tuque that had accompanied Jacques Plante since childhood, and had always distinguished him from the other players on the rink.

2

A Funny-Looking Stick and
a Woollen Tuque

Christmas Day was the only time of the year that the Plante family indulged in the luxury of soft drinks. In the morning, there were Christmas stockings – long wool socks filled with apples, oranges, and clear drop-boil candies. Under the Christmas tree, there would always be a few toys that Jacques' father, Xavier Plante, had made himself. In those Depression years, there was no alternative: with a new baby arriving almost every year, a father had to be clever enough to create a little happiness for his children with his own hands. For Xavier, everything one needed in life could be attained by work, and by using one's imagination,

Jacques Plante, the very young goaltender of the Shawinigan Tigers.

and he instilled those two solid principles in Jacques. Perhaps it was his father's greatest gift to him.

On Christmas Day, 1936, a hockey stick appeared under the tree, although it didn't exactly look like the sticks used by Aurèle Joliat or Howie Morenz (who were both playing their last season in the NHL) to pass and shoot, score goals, and drive the crowd wild. It was a quite different type of stick: a goaltender's stick.

In Shawinigan, at least in his neighbourhood, Jacques was the only child who already possessed a goalie's stick; his father had made it for him from the root of a large tree. But now that he was seven, things were more serious: the boy had to have the regulation wide-bladed stick. Xavier Plante had also made leg pads for Jacques by stuffing potato sacks and reinforcing them with thin wooden panels. Jacques had come home too often with bruised legs after being hit by frozen tennis balls during memorable schoolyard games. The pads were necessary for greater comfort, for Jacques Plante was determined to become a professional hockey player. He had already begun to nurture a dream that he would never abandon, working unstintingly to achieve it, as he would to achieve all of his subsequent ambitions.

Jacques was the eldest of eleven children, and, as in all large families in those days, the eldest was expected to help out at home. Washing floors, or even changing diapers, was no mystery to Jacques. Neither was knitting.

Jacques spent so much time on the skating rink across the street from his home that his ears would get extremely cold. When he told his mother that he needed a tuque, Madame Plante, already overloaded with housework, had answered, "You'll have to knit it yourself."

She gave her son some knitting needles, and patiently taught him how to make his own tuque. The surprising result of this episode was that Jacques began knitting everything he needed: tuques, socks, scarves, and woollen underwear. He liked knitting so much that he taught himself to embroider as well, with remarkable skill.

As it was impossible to knit shoes, the Plante children went barefoot throughout the summer. They were not the only shoeless ones in those days: as soon as the weather was warm enough, all the kids in the neighbourhood would run about barefoot, to their delight. They pitied the children of a better-off family down the street: imagine, the poor kids' feet were imprisoned in shoes even in the middle of the summer!

At school, Jacques did well, succeeding easily both in the classroom and with his homework. But the hockey rink was also part of his school life, situated as it was in the middle of the schoolyard. It was in the centre of town, and was the centre of Jacques' world.

When ice time was taken up by the school hockey team, Jacques would stand against the boards, his tuque pulled well down on his forehead and his goal-tending equipment slung over his shoulder. Jacques Plante was never able to play any other position in hockey because his asthma prevented him from skating for any length of time.

Completely absorbed, he watched the older boys play, analysing each one's strengths and weaknesses.

He wanted to play too, of course; he was just waiting to be noticed. For years, he had been stopping hard tennis balls and pucks. He could skate well. He had already figured out dozens of ways to stop the puck without sending it back to the opponents.

Jacques' opportunity came on a cold, memorable afternoon after school. The "big guys' club," the school team, was practising. His toes numb inside his skates, Jacques shivered with cold as he hung onto the boards. He wouldn't have missed seeing the practice for anything in the world. Suddenly, there was an altercation between the coach and the boy tending the net. Jacques couldn't hear what they were saying, but it was clear that the coach had a lot to get off his chest, and he wasn't listening to any excuses. With an imperious gesture, he ordered the goalie off the ice.

Jacques didn't care what the argument was about – it wasn't his business. The only thing that interested him was the empty net. He waited a moment longer until the coach passed in front of him, then he called out, "Can I replace the goalie?"

The man looked surprised, and for good reason: Jacques was only twelve, while the members of the school team were all sixteen or seventeen years old. He looked around: wasn't anyone else available besides this youngster? There was no time to discuss it, however: the boy was already making his way over to the abandoned net as fast as he could skate.

Jacques had just set out on the path that would lead him to the National Hockey League. Instinctively, he understood that to get ahead in life, one had to be quick on the uptake, to be the right person in the right place at the right time. A goaltender must be more aware of this than anyone else; he should make it his motto. Jacques had just taken advantage of his first big break.

That day, he not only stayed in the nets until the end of practice, but he impressed the coach so much that he stayed there until the end of the season. He became the school's number 1 goalie. He was doing what he loved best: stopping pucks and playing hockey. Alert and intelligent, he was already defending the net with the tenacity of someone who is determined to win.

But Jacques wanted much more. School games were just the first step on a long, ascending stairway.

Two years later, another sterling opportunity came his way. Jacques had never been inside the Shawinigan hockey arena: the entry fee was ten cents, too expensive for his meagre means. But even though he couldn't watch the games, it didn't mean that he would never play there himself. Once again, he called upon his creative imagination. With his equipment slung on his back, Jacques would wait patiently at the entrance of the arena. One day when an intermediate category team arrived to practise, he immediately noticed that there was only one goaltender. He boldly offered his services to the coach: "I can tend one of the nets during the practice."

The man smiled. "Are you sure you can block my boys' shots?"

"*Cercueil!*[1] I've been playing in nets for seven years! You won't lose anything by trying me out."

---

1. *Cercueil*, which means "coffin" in French, is a mild, rather archaic expression that Jacques Plante used often, favouring it over sacriligious or obscene expletives.

The coach gave in – why not give him a try, after all? The kid was skinny, but he was quite tall for his age, and he seemed so determined.

A few minutes later, watching the new recruit in action, the coach found himself wondering if he wouldn't use this Jacques Plante as goaltender in a game. The kid stopped everything that came his way at the practice. The coach was ready to swear that the lanky teenager was only happy when a puck was flying at him. Jacques' eyes never left the black rubber projectile, even for a split second. It was as if he wanted to hypnotize it, tame it. Even the arena manager came to watch from behind the goal zone. After a while, he declared that if this tall boy wasn't an exceptional talent, he didn't know anything about hockey. He told Jacques to come to the arena whenever he wanted to; the side door would always be open to him.

And Jacques dreamed. The lights over the ice glowed: a game had just started. He jumped onto the ice and skated straight over to his net. He felt two thousand pairs of eyes watching him from the stands. He blocked every shot, exactly as if he were wearing the red, white, and blue sweater of the Canadiens, his favourite team. No one had ever actually taught him goaltending; he had only studied photographs and observed the games between the older boys – and had invented his own style.

After a while, there were only a few curious onlookers left in the stands. But Jacques imagined a roar of applause. He observed every last detail of play, and could describe an entire game if he was given the opportunity.

The arena began filling up with curious spectators who came to see how the young prodigy was faring. Soon, Jacques was playing in four different leagues simultaneously, in four different categories: midget, juvenile, junior, and intermediate. He also played for the team of the factory near his home.

One evening, his father, who had found time to attend one of Jacques' factory games, asked him: "Did you know that the players on this team are paid?"

Jacques was astonished.

"*Cercueil!* They're lucky, getting money to play hockey!"

"No, Jacques, they're not paid to play games. But they get a salary by working at the factory. You don't work there, but it's thanks to you that they're winning their games."

Poverty sometimes makes people bold, and Jacques possessed a good measure of audacity. After the game, he approached the team manager and told him that if he wanted to keep his star goalie, he would have pay him a salary. The man was about to refuse indignantly, but he thought it over for a moment and realized that his team's popularity was at risk. He looked around to make sure no one was listening, then said in an undertone: "All right, I'll pay you. I can offer you fifty cents a game, but on one condition."

"What?"

"That you don't tell anyone about it."

Fifty cents a game! For a lad who could enjoy soft drinks only at Christmastime, it was an enormous sum, a small fortune. Jacques accepted the proposed rate, and the condition as well.

Soon, it seemed to Jacques that the stands were always packed. This was no illusion: during the many games that he played in the Shawinigan arena, the spectators had come to appreciate his talent. Jacques received several hockey offers: eighty dollars a week to play in England, and almost as much to play for the Providence Reds in the American Hockey League.

For Jacques' parents, in spite of their difficult financial situation, it was important that their eldest son finish high school before setting out on a hockey career. In any case, even with his passion for the game, Jacques had never neglected his schoolwork. In June, 1947, he obtained his high school diploma with top honours. The year before, he had passed a typing course "with excellence;" he could type 76 words a minute, which probably made him the fastest athlete in the world – on an Underwood keyboard!

After finishing school, Jacques took a job as a clerk in a Shawinigan factory. When he was invited to take part in the Junior Canadiens training camp, he simply took a two-week holiday from work. His boss, Mr. Racette, drove him to Montreal. After his first week at the camp, the Junior Canadiens wanted to keep him on the team, but manager Frank Selke offered him only fifteen dollars a week.

"Fifteen dollars? That's impossible. My room and board costs twenty dollars a week. *Cercueil!* My father can't pay for me to play here, after all!"

Jacques returned to his job in Shawinigan. A few weeks later, the Quebec Citadels offered him eighty-five dollars a week to play for them. It was only

130 kilometres from Quebec City to Shawinigan; Jacques reasoned that he would not be too far away from home, and therefore would not be too homesick in a strange town. He accepted.

At eighteen, Jacques Plante already showed that he had a good head for business. And hockey was in his blood.

∞

Chicago, April 4, 1953.

The 15,834 people in the Stadium were keeping up their overwhelming booing of the Canadiens. The Chicago hockey fans, who had not been spoiled by watching their team win the Stanley Cup many times over, were reputed to be the loudest, most unruly ones in the NHL. And they knew that Montreal was the team to beat.

When the Habs had lost at the Montreal Forum on the previous Thursday, Montreal fans showed their discontent by repeatedly littering the ice with rubber overshoes, hats, and rolled-up hockey programmes. In Montreal, a defeat was always a dramatic incident. The home-town partisans in Chicago seemed determined to show that they could be just as rowdy.

Jacques skated over to the net amid a swelling chorus of jeers. The ice seemed soft under his skates and his legs felt like jelly.

Referee Red Storey dropped the puck onto the ice for the first face-off. From the start, it was clear that it was going to be a rough game. The Black Hawks in their darker, home-ice sweaters had no intention of yielding an inch of territory. To a man, they were ready to fight.

In the third minute of play, Jim McFadden, the top scorer for the Hawks, broke away from the Habs defence. Spurred on by the screaming fans, he tried a feint. Jacques saw it coming and stopped the puck. Thirty seconds later, to the surprise of everyone in the stadium, he left his crease to retrieve the puck and passed it to the young Canadien defenceman, Dollard St. Laurent. Jacques had set the tone for the match.

He felt better already. In Chicago and anywhere else in the hockey world, the rink was his territory. He was part of the show, and took his cue as one of the star actors.

Jacques Plante excels in other sports
besides hockey, especially baseball.

3

Far from Home...and from the Nets

During the first games of the 1947-1948 season, the fans at the Quebec Coliseum were avidly cheering for the Citadels, the Junior League team that they supported throughout the year. It was a mediocre team with a weak defensive line. Luckily, this year there was a talented rookie who showed great promise: Jacques Plante, the goalie with the tuque on his head. He was the player who limited the worst of the damage. But could he take the Citadels to the finals?

Plante was spectacular at blocking difficult shots, but it was his practice of roving from the net that captured the fans' imagination. Several times during every game, they would rise from their seats, holding their

breath, as Jacques, nicknamed "the Rover," left the net
to retrieve a loose puck and pass it to one of his teammates. One evening, Jacques, who unfailingly rose to a
challenge, even jumped backward over his net to get a
puck that had stopped behind the goal cage, and did it
successfully. The fans could hardly believe their eyes;
they applauded thunderously before they settled down
into their seats again, their hearts beating in excitement. With this kind of derring-do showmanship,
Jacques Plante was already an expert in giving the audi-
ence their money's worth in thrills and chills.

Fans with a more progressive outlook declared
that he was a genius, while the more conservative partisans grumbled doubtfully. But no one could remain
indifferent to his revolutionary style, which was as
effective as it was spectacular.

Some amateur managers loudly advised him to
stay in the net. The goalkeeper, concentrating as usual
on what was happening in the neutral zone, could hear
them. But he knew that as soon as another loose puck
came into the home zone, he would be impelled to
skate out of the goal crease to avert the danger.

Sometimes, it was only to get a puck that was shot
from far down the ice into the corner. But what made
people nervous was when Jacques would go even farther
out of his net to race an opponent to the puck – an opponent who could skate faster and was less encumbered
than he was. Despite his heavy equipment, Jacques
almost always came out the winner in these contests.

At the Coliseum, this kind of thing had never been
seen before – neither in Quebec City nor anywhere else
where organized hockey was played. It was a radical

departure from the orthodox view that the goalkeeper must stay in his net and let his teammates recover the puck. But this young goalie had analysed all the facets of the game and had coolly reached the logical conclusion that as long as he controlled the puck, the opponents could not shoot at his net. In his own special way, Jacques brought sparks into the atmosphere.

Many of the fans obviously thought that it was largely a matter of grandstanding. But if they had been able to see the game from the goaltender's point of view, they would have understood why he did it. Jacques never left the net just to amuse himself, or to tease the crowd. His actions were based strictly on a strategy of self-defence: he was simply saving his skin – and his career.

From the very first practice of the season, Jacques had carefully observed his defencemen. He knew that one of them couldn't skate backwards, one never shot the puck past his own blue-line, one could only turn around in one direction, another was strong but slow on his feet, and so on. If he didn't want to find himself in trouble all the time and have to continually duel alone with opponents who had been allowed to approach the nets unimpeded, his only choice was to get right into the game and to rove all over his zone.

In spite of the heart-stopping moments that he gave them, the Citadels fans could not resist going to see the sensational goalie in action. Jacques became the star attraction of the season, and, according to sportswriters, "the hottest prospect in the League." That year, with 22 games played at home, the Citadels attracted a record number of more than 100,000 spectators.

By the season's end, Jacques was playing so well that the Citadels beat the Junior Canadiens in the finals. Sam Pollock, responsible for developing new players for the Montreal Canadiens, was impressed. "It was Jacques Plante who beat us," he confided to a newspaper reporter.

It was true. Jacques was even named the most valuable player – and by a long shot – on his team.

Canadiens manager Frank Selke was now convinced. He wanted Jacques to be part of the organization, unconditionally. He knew that the Toronto Maple Leafs had already included Jacques' name on a list of possible recruits. He also knew that Roland Mercier, the Rangers scout, was doing his best to entice the young Cerberus to play in New York.

"You'll be much better off with us," Mercier told Jacques. "Think about it. In Montreal, the Canadiens already have Bill Durnan. And there's the Royals' Gerry McNeil, just itching to put on his pads. He's only a little older than you and he still has a long career ahead of him."

But Jacques hesitated. Could he possibly turn down the possibility of playing for the Montreal Canadiens? He had always imagined himself in red, white and blue...

"With Toronto, it would be just as hard," continued the wily Mercier. "They've won the Stanley Cup four years running. Turk Broda is at the peak of his form. With us, there will only be Chuck Rayner to dethrone."

Jacques needed time to think these arguments over.

During the two years that he played for the Citadels in junior hockey, Jacques, with the help of the enthusiastic hockey lovers of Quebec City, was steadily gaining confidence in his abilities, and frequently wondered if he shouldn't try his luck with a big league team other than the Montreal Canadiens. He carefully studied the sports pages in the newspapers. He reflected, while cutting out pictures of his idols to put in his scrapbooks.

The heroes preserved on these pages were the great athletes of the day: wrestling champion Yvon Robert; the two right-wingers, Maurice Richard and Gordie Howe; Mickey Mantle, smiling on the day he hit a phenomenal 200-metre home run; Terry Sawchuk, the goaltender of the AHL Indianapolis Caps, when he was named outstanding rookie of the 1948-1949 season; boxers Joe Louis, who still struck fear into the hearts of his rivals; and Marcel Cerdan, who had just died in an airplane crash. Interspersed among these sports giants were illustrious figures from the entertainment world, including French actor Bourvil, whose humour Jacques loved, and Hollywood's latest version of Frankenstein!

Jacques filled other scrapbooks with newspaper clippings of his own exploits in hockey and in the other sports he practised: winning the Player of the Year Award in the Shawinigan Industrial Softball League in the summer of 1948, and his successes as a player in the Lévis Baseball League in the summer of 1949.

Jacques loved all sports and was insatiably curious about life. But he never wavered from his main ambition:

to play for the Habs, the team revered by all French Canadians. He was reluctant to move far from the heart of the hockey world. Besides, his command of English was not yet solid, and he had just married Jacqueline Gagné, whom he had met in Quebec City in October, 1948.

Frank Selke contacted Jacques again. It was taken for granted that the best hockey players from Quebec belonged to the Montreal Canadiens. Mr. Selke made it a point to continue this tradition.

∽

Chicago, April 4, 1953.

After six minutes of play, Dickie Moore made a brilliant pass to Bernie Geoffrion, who found himself alone in front of the net. Al Rollins made the save, but Boom-Boom managed to reach the rebounding puck and tipped it past the Hawks' goalie.

A few seconds later, referee Red Storey was obliged to halt play when Tom Johnson was hit by an egg. The Chicago fans were throwing down eggs, paper airplanes, coins, and water bags. They imagined that by imitating the Canadiens fans at the Forum, they would "egg" their team on to victory. It took the arena maintenance workers a considerable time to clean off the ice.

Leaning on the crossbar of his net, Jacques Plante was soaking in the atmosphere of fierce competition that reigned among NHL teams during the playoffs. The young goaltender was feeling better every minute that passed. He was always at his best when the challenge was difficult.

4

Behind the Bench with the Habs

F rank Selke was like a father to many members of
the Canadiens hockey club. He had close relation-
ships with his best players. He also possessed the con-
summate art of making the team understand the reasons behind his decisions. This man quickly realized
that Jacques Plante was no ordinary goaltender. In
Selke's view, Jacques was not only spectacular in the
nets but was also a very ambitious, intelligent young
man. He had no doubt that the goalie would make his
mark in the major league; Jacques was clearly a winner.
On August 17, 1949, the Habs' general manager went
straight to the point: "Jacques, we believe in your talent, and we want to see you get ahead. You're too old

CLUB DE HOCKEY CANADIEN INC.

Membre de la—National Hockey League—Member
2313 ST. CATHERINE ST. WEST

TEL. WILBANK 6131

MONTREAL,

June 23rd, 1948.

To: Jacques Plante

Dear Sir;

      Please be advised that we will expect you to report to our Training Camp at St. Hyacinthe with Dallas .... on Sept. 20/48 ...., where you will be given every opportunity to put yourself in tip-top condition for the coming hockey season.

      This early notice is sent you so that you may arrange your plans accordingly. A later reminder will go out about the middle of August. If for any reason you can not attend the Camp, please let us know.

      Transportation and hotel accomodation will be arranged for you at our expense.

Yours very truly,
CLUB DE HOCKEY CANADIEN

Frank J. Selke

FRANK J. SELKE
GENERAL MANAGER

FJS:EA

In September 1948, Jacques Plante is called by General Manager Frank Selke to attend the Canadiens training camp.

to play in the junior league, so I think you'd better stay with us."

Jacques wasn't naïve – he didn't believe for a minute that he was being offered the position of number 1 goaltender for the Canadiens. Although Bill Durnan was thirty-four years old, he had just won his fifth Vézina Trophy in six seasons. He had posted ten shutouts, setting a record with four consecutive shutouts. That meant that he had minded the net for 309 minutes and 21 seconds without letting the other team score. On a slightly lower level, Gerry McNeil was making a brilliant showing for the Royals. Where would Jacques Plante have fit in? But Selke was an old hand at cards and knew when to play his trumps.

"I've decided that Gerry will play for Cincinnati so that he can get to know the players in the American League. You're going to take over for him with the Royals." And, convincing negotiator that he was, Selke added, "You'll be paid $4,500 for the season, plus $500 for practising with the Canadiens."

For a young man whose greatest pleasure was to have pucks shot at him, the offer was attractive – all the more so because this arrangement would allow him to satisfy his insatiable curiosity, develop his playing skill, measure his capabilities, and display his talent. What more could he ask? Every day, he would be measured against the best goalie on ice, Bill Durnan; he would be trying to block shots by the some of the best players of the *bleu-blanc-rouge* machine, including Maurice Richard and Elmer Lach; and at the same time, he would be playing regularly in the Quebec Senior Hockey League.

It was a gift on a silver platter that Jacques could hardly refuse. Frank Selke, for his part, had finagled yet another masterful deal: while keeping the best goalie in the league on his team, he was also keeping the best future goalie at his beck and call.

∞

It did not take long for Jacques to come into his own with the Royals. From the very first games, sportswriters realized that he not only performed his job extremely well but that he also had fresh ideas and expressed them with great conviction. From the beginning, Jacques Plante was a goldmine for the press.

In the Montreal *Gazette* of October 15, 1949, sports fans read:

> The Royals are solid with young Jacques Plante stepping into the shoes left vacant by Gerry McNeil. Plante, who was all-star goalie with the Quebec Citadels last year, is considered the third-best goalie in the Canadiens' vast hockey organization. He is definite major league timber...

And right from the start, Jacques' name was in the headlines:

La Presse, October 17, 1949:

THE SENIOR LEAGUE ROYALS OPEN
THEIR LOCAL SEASON WITH A
VICTORY OVER OTTAWA

Jacques Plante was brilliant in the nets.

Eleven days later, in *La Patrie*:

THE ROYALS WIN THEIR SECOND
VICTORY IN TWO DAYS.
Jacques Plante: *extraordinaire*!

Into the first month of the season, on October 28th, Jacques was named "Star of the Week" by *La Presse*, an honour usually reserved for NHL players.

A TIP OF THE HAT TO THE STAR
OF THE WEEK: JACQUES PLANTE
We had to delve into the ranks of the Senior League this week to find the athlete who deserved the honour of the Tip of the Hat. More specifically, we had to go to the Royals camp to find our hero. He wears a tuque, a forgotten ornament in the game of hockey since the days of Georges Vézina. His name is Jacques Plante.
    This young man excelled in the two victories won by his team away from home on Wednesday and Thursday evenings. It seems that, by his prowess, the young Quebecker will make us forget about Gerry McNeil's departure for Cincinnati. So, again we say "Bravo!" for his masterful job in the Royals' net.

That year, Bill Durnan won his sixth Vézina Trophy. A record — one that Jacques would store in his mind. He was aiming for even greater heights.

∞

Jacques was overwhelmingly curious, and when he was not on the road with the Royals, he loved to hang around the Forum, especially when the Canadiens' opponents were practising before a game. The Detroit Red Wings did not recognize the young man sitting in the stands behind Terry Sawchuk's cage on some of those mornings. Jacques would observe the star goalie's every move: the famous crouch that Jacques had already adopted and which allowed him to keep sight of the puck at all times, even when a scramble occurred in front of the net; Sawchuk's way of positioning the wide blade of his stick to take up as much space as possible; his lateral slide to intercept a shot with perfect timing.

During his first season in the NHL, Terry Sawchuk had worked wonders. He had posted shutout after shutout, maintaining a goals-against average of under 2 per game. He had won the Calder Trophy, awarded to the outstanding rookie of the year, and had missed winning the Vézina Trophy by a single point. Terry Sawchuk would continue to perform miracles and would take the Red Wings to win the Stanley Cup that year.

Still relatively unknown, Jacques Plante progressed with stubborn tenacity and tireless enthusiasm.

In their practice sessions, the Canadiens often played against the Royals, at a time when Maurice Richard was about to become the highest scorer in hockey history. Jacques soon understood why the Rocket was able to score so many goals: during practices, as much as in the games themselves, he viewed the goaltender as an enemy to be defeated, at any cost. The Rocket never shot the puck with anything less than his full strength: he always shot to score.

When Elmer Lach went to retrieve the puck in the left corner of the offensive zone and pass it to his right-winger, The Rocket, Jacques would slide to his left, and Maurice would invariably shoot into the right-hand corner of the net. One day, Maurice took the time to explain. "It's quite simple. When I get a pass from the corner, I know that you'll slide to the opposite side. Normally, you'd have a better chance of stopping the shot that way. But I aim for the place you were when the pass was made. Because you're already into your slide, I usually get it in."

This strategy was tailor-made for Richard, who usually shot from the left because it gave him a wider angle. While Jacques was digesting what Maurice had said, the legendary right-winger was silent for a moment, then chuckled. "Frankly, Jacques, I shouldn't give you any advice. I never really know how I'm going to shoot the puck. So, ask yourself: if I don't know where I'm going to aim until the last second, how do you expect the goaltender to know? That's why I score so many goals."

Jacques possessed the patience of truly curious people. He never passed up an opportunity to improve his goaltending skills.

His popularity increased with every game. His job with the Royals took him all over the province of Quebec, and in every town, his daredevil style and his spectacular saves were a prime attraction. Jacques was developing along with several other young players who were also waiting for their big chance to break into the NHL. There was the speedy Dollard St. Laurent, a defenceman who was always quick to go on the offensive when the occasion arose, and there was Dickie Moore, the left-winger who, people said, had a compass in his head.

Frank Carlin, the Royals' coach, had nothing but praise for his goaltender, as Jacques had built up a big lead over all the rival teams. Toe Blake, who coached the Valleyfield Braves at this time, also took note of his astonishing performances. Whether it was in Quebec City, Chicoutimi, Shawinigan, Sherbooke, or Ottawa, Jacques Plante drew large crowds. He shared the spotlight in the Senior League circuit with another exceptional talent: Jean Béliveau, who played centre for the Quebec City Aces.

The more Jacques' prowess came to the fore, the more press reports were dedicated to him, particularly in the Montreal dailies. In *La Presse*, Maurice Desjardins, the columnist who wrote a feature called "*Tous les sports*," revealed an aspect of the goaltender's personality that few people were aware of:

> THE HIDDEN TALENTS
> OF JACQUES "TUQUE" PLANTE
> The brilliant Royals goaltender is a past master of the art of...knitting and embroidery.
> "Colour" is one of the important attributes of anyone who wants to carve out a career in professional sports. I give you the examples of Maurice Richard, Bernard Geoffrion,

Johnny Greco, and Sam Jethoe, who all possess a remarkable degree of that special something that electrifies crowds and brings them to games in droves. I think that Jacques Plante, the acrobatic goaltender of the Senior League Royals, is a naturally "colourful" athlete in action and one who manages to stay colourful even after the game is over!...

He spends all his leisure time drawing, and – keep your hats on – knitting and doing embroidery....

You've got to see Plante in the train car that carries the Royals, dexterously picking up a stitch while his teammates play Hearts....

By the way, he knits all of his famous tuques himself. We asked him if he had decided to imitate Georges Vézina's well-known mania. "Not at all," he told us. "*Maman* used to make me wear them when I played for the Collège St. Maurice on the outdoor rink in Shawinigan."

Jacques Plante is the kind of young athlete who wants to try everything and who succeeds in everything he does.

Besides these eminently original touches, Jacques was fully convinced that he would eventually move up to play for the Habs. He was even more certain of it when Bill Durnan, the amazing ambidextrous goalie, suddenly announced his retirement at the end of the 1949-1950 hockey season. Durnan was replaced by Gerry McNeil.

⟨∞⟩

January, 1953.

Back in Frank Selke's office, Jacques knew that the club was counting on him. At the end of October, Dick Irvin had brought Jacques up to replace Gerry McNeil, who had fractured his jaw. He tended the Canadiens' nets for three games – three games that were marked by two heavily publicized episodes.

First, Maurice Richard had unsuccessfully attempted to score the two goals remaining for him to surpass Nels Stewart's all-time NHL record of 324 career goals. However, for Jacques, these games were memorable for another event: the unforgettable Battle of the Tuque.

The sports world is heavily imbued with all sorts of superstitions. When a team wins a string of consecutive victories, some coaches don't want the players to change their uniforms so as not to break the lucky streak. Somewhat in the same spirit, Jacques believed his success was partly due to the good luck charm that had always accompanied him in his career: his woollen tuque. Dick Irvin, however, did not want any of his players to stand out by any addition to their regular uniforms. "There's a National League rule that forbids the wearing of tuques during games," Irvin told Jacques. In fact, the cunning Silver Eagle had just invented this regulation.

Jacques was ready with a quick reply: "Aurèle Joliat always played with his cap on. He would never have played a game without it."

But the coach had another argument: "I'm sure that if Jacques Plante lost his tuque at a crucial moment, he'd stoop to pick it up and forget about the puck. I wouldn't want that kind of thing to happen."

The reporters were delighted. Again, Jacques was giving them good material for a story. They were already comparing him to Georges Vézina in their articles.

Irvin hadn't given up. We will never know whether he himself or one of his assistants was the culprit, but sure enough, right before Jacques' first game tending the Habs' net, all three of his tuques vanished from the Royals' dressing room. He was obliged to play for the Canadiens without his security blanket – three games, three victories, with only four goals scored against him.

Although columnist Jean Séguin wrote "Jacques Plante without his tuque is like a hot-dog without mustard," the young goaltender was forced to acknowledge that he could play just as well without his famous headgear as with it. He even told Maurice Richard that if The Rocket scored his 325th goal, he would be happy to give him his favourite tuque as a prize. In the end, even without the tuque, Jacques demonstrated that he was of NHL calibre.

When Frank Selke called him into his office at the beginning of 1953, Jacques knew that the manager had something important to say. "Jacques, we're more than satisfied by your performance with the Royals. I have to admit it: you were instrumental in the team's success."

Jacques was all ears. He sensed that he was about to enter another phase of his career and come a step closer to achieving his dream. Selke continued: "Now I have others plans for you. You're well-known in Quebec now, and very, very popular, as we are fully aware. But it would be good for you to go a step further. The Americans don't know you yet; you've got to show them what you can do. They'll appreciate your talent in the States; I'm convinced they're going to love your style. Then, when you do start in the NHL, the players are going to be more intimidated by the exploits of a Jacques Plante whom they've heard of, rather than a Jacques Plante who is just a rookie from the Quebec Senior League."

This time, Jacques did not hesitate – it was a chance to add another plume to his hat and to gain more experience. He signed on the bottom line of the new contract, and, accompanied by his wife and their little boy, Michel, he set off to play for the Canadiens' U.S. farm-club team in Buffalo.

∞

Fred Hunt, general manager of the Buffalo Bisons, and the player-coach, Frank Eddolls, were all smiles. Their team, after starting the season off slowly, had suddenly taken off. The two men began to believe in magic and hoped they weren't in for a rude awakening. Since the arrival of their new goaltender, Buffalo hadn't lost a single game!

Hunt picked up the telephone. He had a report to make to Kenny Reardon, the Canadiens' recruiting manager. "You know, Ken, Plante's only minded the nets for four games, and everyone in the league's talking about him. He's the biggest attraction since the good old days of Terry Sawchuk."

"We knew he was good," Reardon conceded.

"Good? That's not the word for it! He's miraculous!"

Deep inside, Fred Hunt wondered if he should be talking about Jacques so enthusiastically. What if the Canadiens decided to call him up right away? Fortunately for the Bisons, Gerry McNeil was having an extraordinary season in the Habs' net. The Canadiens had nothing to worry about as far as goalminding was concerned – and even if a problem did arise, there was little Charlie Hodge, who was making a name for himself in the minors.

"With a bit of luck," continued Hunt, "Plante would have had four shutouts. When he was outplayed in Cleveland, in the middle of the first period of his first game in the League, it was Frank Eddolls who got the puck into the net. And last Sunday, he stopped Jackie Gordon's shot, but a teammate, Kobbussen, scored when he was trying to get the puck out of the home zone."

All told, Jacques had kept the puck out of the net for 217 minutes and 54 seconds between those two goals. The reporters covering the American League games knew how to spell his name by now.

"But that isn't all," added Hunt. "Last Sunday, there were nine thousand people at the game. Next week, when we play against the Pittsburgh Hornets, we're expecting an even bigger crowd."

Frank Eddolls was equally optimistic. With Jacques Plante in front of the net, he nurtured hopes of the Bisons reaching the finals.

After a few games, Jacques became the reporters' darling. They gave him the nickname that would stick throughout his career: Jake the Snake.

∞

Chicago, April 4, 1953.

In the second period, Maurice Richard skated around the net to shoot against Al Rollins. The goaltender made the save, but the puck ricocheted off defenceman Gus Morton's leg and went into the net. A lucky goal, of course, but when you're a top scorer, luck is often on your side.

Three minutes before the end of the period, Ken Mosdell scored the third Habs' goal on passes by Lorne Davis and Calum MacKay. Jacques Plante, showing incredible cool-headedness, blocked all twenty shots by the Hawks. Thanks to him, his coach's prediction came true: the Canadiens won 3-0. Jacques had risen to the occasion. Dick Irvin Senior had taken a risk and it had paid off.

The cunning old fox realized that every time he sent Jacques Plante into a game, his team was victorious. Two days later, Irvin sent him into the mêlée again. The result was a 4-1 win for the bleu-blanc-rouge.

At the end of the game, the heroes of his dreams surrounded the young goaltender to congratulate him. Chicago was eliminated. Jacques had just carried off his first exploit in the NHL.

He minded the nets during the first two games of the finals against the Boston Bruins, a 4-2 victory and a loss by the same count. Gerry McNeil reclaimed his place for the following games, and the Canadiens won the Stanley Cup.

It was the first time that Jacques Plante's name was engraved on the famous trophy, the emblem of world supremacy on ice; it would not be the last.

∞

Everyone knew that Jacques had been instrumental in these wins. His style was original. He went outside his goal crease whenever he felt like it, as if he wanted to frighten the fans and his coach. But it was obvious that he would be the Canadiens' next number 1 goalie – it was just a question of time.

Jacques, who was referred to in the American League as "the saviour of the Canadiens in 1953," remained in that league for almost another whole season. He was finally called up to join the Canadiens on February 12, 1954.

To meet the ultimate challenge and to mount the podium, it only remained for Jacques Plante to show that he was the best. That season, he tended goal in 17 games, maintaining a goals-against average of 1.59 per game.

Frank Selke called him into his office, and told him bluntly, "Jacques, you've got the job."

"*Cercueil*, I'm so happy!" was Jacques' ecstatic reply.

He had definitely not obtained the position under any false pretences, and he would give his employers more than their money's worth. His period of glory was just beginning.

Second Period

A Masked Knight
in the Kingdom of Hockey

Maurice "The Rocket" Richard,
the Canadiens' phenomenal star forward from 1942 to 1961.

5

The Rocket's World

B y the end of the 1953-1954 hockey season, Jacques
Plante had worked his way up, step by step, into
the National League, by dint of his ability, his tenacity,
his intelligence, and above all, his strong sense of perfectionism – all necessary qualities for those who want
to achieve success in professional sports, especially
those who aim for stardom in their respective fields.
Jacques stood out sharply from other rookie goalies by
his frequent sorties beyond the goal crease and by his
way of analysing and reacting to all the aspects of play
during a game. Now that the objective he had sought
for so long was in his grasp, he knew that he must be
careful to keep luck on his side.

Aware and alert as he was, Jacques knew all too well where his major weakness lay: in his left hand. When he fell off a ladder and fractured his wrist when he was five years old, the bones did not set properly. This meant that he could never swivel his hand completely outward to catch high shots. He compensated for this by using the rest of his body: he would quickly lift his leg to wedge the puck between his thigh and his arm. However, he realized that in the NHL, nothing was as easy as in the minors. The best forwards were astute at studying their opponents' playing styles, detecting weak points to take advantage of. Also, the shots were so much faster that Jacques was afraid he might not have the same blocking ability that he had shown in the minors. For these reasons, he decided to undergo corrective surgery to his wrist in the spring of 1954.

On the day of the operation, Jacques' curiosity – the same curiosity that had led him to invent hundreds of tricks of the trade in a domain where there were no qualified teachers – played a nasty trick on him. He felt uneasy in the operating room: he didn't like the idea of the surgeon being free to play around with his hand, particularly when his entire future depended on it. He asked to have a local instead of a general anesthetic so that he could see what the doctor was doing. It seemed that Jacques Plante had nerves of steel!

However, as soon as he saw the surgeon cut into his flesh, he began to feel dizzy. After a few moments, his eyes rolled upward and he turned his face away. In the end, he had to undergo a total anesthetic for the rest of the procedure. Despite the large number of injuries that he sustained during his career, Jacques could never bear the sight of blood. It frightened him, and that day, he learned that it was impossible to completely eliminate his fear. But he also discovered the importance of managing fear and turning it into an ally.

Jacques was a sensitive man. He was a persevering athlete and could be very hard on himself, but he also had a vulnerable side. His strength lay in the fact that he always rose to a challenge as a means of overcoming pressure. It was the only way to scale the heights defined by his ambition, and he knew it. His emotional nature occasionally led him into difficulty, but it was in this very vulnerability that he found the strength to fight on.

Montreal has always been the flashpoint of emotions in the hockey world. As soon as the weather starts to get chilly, all talk turns to the coming season. The eyes of every fan in the province are trained expectantly on their idols, nicknamed *les Glorieux*. Their heroes' exploits make the harsh Canadian winter tolerable – even desirable. Fans in the cities and in small towns lost in ice and snow join in a common bond, criticizing the Canadiens' defeats and noisily applauding their victories. Ordinary people like to express their opinions on developments in hockey more than on any other aspect of life. Naturally, they want their team to win. They want the winter to be red, white, and blue, and the sun to bounce its rays off the Stanley Cup in the springtime.

The Canadiens' management was obliged to pick the most talented players; they couldn't afford to make a mistake. The slightest error in judgment always resulted in screaming headlines in the sports pages the next morning. In this demanding context, Jacques was enormously relieved when it became clear that his operation had been an unqualified success. From then on, he could catch pucks in his left glove as well as any other goalie in the League – an essential requirement, since there were only six goaltending positions in the NHL, and only one for the Habs.

The hockey goalkeeper is constantly under enormous pressure. Ultimately, he is a lone figure amongst his teammates – the most solitary among the stalwarts. Besides the fear of being outplayed and the fear of injury, he also has to contend with the fear of letting his teammates down, of destroying team morale if he lets in an easy shot or fails to make a crucial save – more often than not, the save that would make up for someone else's error. He knows that the fans' eyes are focused mainly on the goaltender. He is the one who is at the greatest risk of losing his position on the team. This was more true in the 1950s than in any other era of hockey. The net custodian would only leave his post for one of two reasons: if he was injured, or if the coach wasn't satisfied with his showing.

The Canadiens of 1954-1955, as everyone knew, could tap into a rich fount of netminding talent. If Jacques Plante was to prove that he was a worthy successor to Bill Durnan by taking Gerry McNeil's place, he only had 52 matches to do it in.

Thus, in spite of the indisputable exploits that Jacques had accomplished since replacing McNeil, Dick Irvin did not hesitate to remind him that the club had other talented pretenders waiting in the wings. For a few games, Jacques had to move over for little Charlie Hodge, who was also anxious to prove himself.

Irvin's tactic appeared to be a kind of cattle prod, as if he wanted to stimulate Jacques in this manner. Jacques had to steel himself to hold on, continue to improve, stay cool, and show his mettle in every game.

It wasn't easy wearing a Canadiens uniform, but for Jacques, it was the price of a dream come true.

∞

The most memorable event in Jacques Plante's first complete season with the Habs occurred on March 17, 1955, when a riot at the Montreal Forum shook an entire society. The riot not only upset the hockey world and the Canadiens, it also affected the political consciousness of the whole province of Quebec.

The spark that set off this chain of events occurred on Sunday, March 13, in Boston. The game pitting the Habs against the Bruins was important. The playoffs were fast approaching; with only four regular games left, the Canadiens had to work hard if they wanted to edge past the Detroit Red Wings, who led by four points in the NHL standings. Jacques was in the nets. Rocket Richard, who had scored his 400th career goal a little earlier in the season, was going all out to achieve an objective that he had always strived for: winning the scoring title of the National League regular season. Although he was the highest all-time point-getter in the League's history and held a slew of individual records, he hadn't yet achieved that particular one. The Rocket was leading teammates Bernard Geoffrion and Jean Béliveau by two and three points respectively in the standings for top scorer.

The game was getting rough. Because the rink of the Boston Garden was smaller than those of other hockey cities, there was a tendency toward more forceful bodychecks and more frequent skirmishes on the ice. In those days, a game in Boston often ended up looking like trench warfare.

In the first period, Hal Laycoe administered a hard check to Richard, and was given a penalty for charging. In the third period, the Bruins were leading 4 to 1. When defenceman Warren Godfrey was taken out for a penalty in the thirteenth minute, Dick Irvin decided to go for all or nothing. He called Jacques out of the game and sent in six players, hoping to overpower the Boston defence. They were: Harvey, Johnson, Béliveau, Olmstead, Geoffrion, and Maurice Richard. A few seconds later, Johnson was replaced by Jackie Leclair. Irvin still kept Jacques out, even if the face-off was in the Canadiens' zone. The Habs tore towards the Bruins' net. Laycoe, seeing that The Rocket was outskating him, slashed him on the head with his stick, laying open a deep cut under his hair.

The Rocket, dizzy and holding his head in his hands, went over to show the evidence to the referee, Frank Udvari, and demanded a major penalty for Laycoe. The referee refused. Richard realized that he was bleeding profusely. Never one to restrain himself in the heat of the action, he grabbed a stick and hit Laycoe on the back, then punched him in the face, opening a wound over his right eye.

The crowd went wild. Doug Harvey and the other Habs tried to hold The Rocket back. A young linesman, Cliff Thompson, grabbed onto the famous number 9 sweater from behind. Meanwhile, Laycoe took up his stick and went for Richard. The enraged Rocket ordered the linesman to let him go, but Thompson held on for dear life. Maurice then lost his temper completely, wrested himself free, and socked Thompson twice. Frank Udvari had no alternative but to order the star right-winger into the dressing room, where club physician Hector Dubois managed to calm him down and give him first-aid treatment. The Bruins won the game 4-2.

Rocket Richard's punishment was not over yet. Two days later, the League president, Clarence Campbell, called Richard, Dick Irvin, and Kenny Reardon into his office in the Sun Life Building. After a few minutes, as if he wanted to make an example of the Canadiens biggest star, he announced that Richard was suspended, not only for the three games remaining in the regular season, but for the playoffs as well! This was a case of flagrant injustice. The radio waves hummed with the news and editorials denounced the suspension as a too-severe punishment, while ordinary Quebeckers grumbled rebelliously. The man in the street, just as much as the most ardent hockey fan, felt instinctively that he should stand up and defend himself. It was intolerable that the sport's greatest idol be humiliated in this high-handed manner.

Before the game between the Red Wings and the Canadiens on March 17th, hundreds of fans unable to obtain tickets began a spontaneous protest outside the Montreal Forum.

Inside the building, it was clear that the Canadiens had been shaken by the suspension: they allowed the Wings to take a 4-1 lead in the first period. In the eleventh minute of play, Clarence Campbell arrived with his fiancée and coolly took his place in his regular seat in the stands. The fans took their mounting frustration out on him: he was immediately pelted with all imaginable kinds of projectiles; he was booed and jostled. Campbell held on to his hat and remained seated. But during the break between periods, the fans' resentment became uncontrollable. A man made his way towards Campbell, extending his arm as if he wanted to shake his hand. At the last moment, the man lunged forward and punched Campbell twice in the face. The League president was obliged to vacate his seat and seek shelter in the Forum's first-aid room, under a hail of eggs, tomatoes, and water bags. Then, an unidentified person exploded a tear-gas bomb, and all hell broke loose.

The game was cancelled. After only one period of play, the win was conceded to the Red Wings, giving them 2 points in the League standings – 2 important points, as it turned out. At the end of the regular season a few days later, the Wings were at the top of the standings, exactly 2 points ahead of the Canadiens.

The hysterical crowd surged onto St. Catherine Street, bellowing and roaring, shattering store windows, overturning cars, and setting fire to anything that would burn. March 17, 1955, is etched in the collective memory as the date of the biggest riot in Quebec's history.

The following day, the mayor of Montreal, Jean Drapeau, made an appeal for calm. Maurice Richard himself spoke on the radio, saying that he had accepted his penalty; he exhorted hockey fans to continue supporting the team, even if he couldn't be with them in their fight to win the League championship and the Stanley Cup.

This episode revealed to Jacques Plante, the Habs' rookie goaltender, what Maurice Richard meant to the people of Quebec. He was their prodigal son; he epitomized their wish to be winners and to rise into the ranks of the best. Jacques' role was not only to mind nets for his dream team: he was also the defender of that symbol of honour and success, the Montreal Canadiens Hockey Club. Only the best could be part of it, and those privileged few had to be totally dedicated to taking it to the top and keeping it there.

A few days later, while tending goal against the New York Rangers, Jacques was initiated to a strange kind of loyalty among sports fans when the crowd booed a goal by Bernie Geoffrion that put him ahead of their idol Richard as top scorer of the season. That summer, Boom Boom was almost ashamed of his achievement. He even received threats by some deluded hockey fans! But, Jacques wondered, when you're playing for the Canadiens, shouldn't you always aim for the top? When opportunity strikes, shouldn't you shoot for a goal? Nonetheless, robbing The Rocket of his cherished record seemed a monstrous act of *lèse-majesté*.

The season ended on a catastrophic note: at the Detroit Olympia, the Habs were defeated by a shameful score of 6-0.

The undaunted Dick Irvin instituted a new technique in the first game of the semifinal series against the Boston Bruins. Determined that the team would not suffer the same humiliating loss that they had in Detroit, he alternated Jacques Plante and Charlie Hodge in the nets. Defensively, the Canadiens played impeccably, and the tandem of goalies posted a shutout with a 2-0 victory. The win was credited to Jacques, who had been on the ice 75 per cent of game time. Irvin tried this arrangement again in the second game, which the *bleu-blanc-rouge* won 3-1. Unfortunately, this system of alternating goaltenders, in spite of its novelty, took away from the respective netminders' concentration. Jacques was happier being the sole goalkeeper of his team for the remainder of the playoffs.

The Canadiens went on to the seventh, sudden-death game of the semifinals and lost to the Red Wings in Detroit. Even without their star right-winger, they had done their best and had performed well. They may have lost at the end, but they would make up for it. The Canadiens would always rise again, because Montreal was not only the centre of the hockey kingdom: it was also the home of the Stanley Cup.

6

A Taste for the Stanley Cup

The dynasty was reborn in 1955-1956: the Canadiens became the League leaders again. A specific group of players, who would reign over their rivals for five consecutive years, constituted the strongest team that had ever been seen in professional hockey, according to respected sports observers. What was their secret? The simple answer was that the team's cohesiveness, talent, strength, hard work, courage, and audacity combined to make it dominate the National League, sometimes by a ludicrous margin.

Hockey requires a high degree of teamwork. The Habs were exemplary in this all-important aspect, showing it game after game. They were dubbed "the

The Canadiens Hockey Club, National League champions and winners of the Stanley Cup (1957-1958 season).

Flying Frenchmen" in the United States. The Montreal Canadiens were synonymous with skating. They never stopped moving on the ice: if they weren't in control of the puck, they went after the opponents. Once they got the puck, they would immediately attack. Their style thrilled the crowds who were repeatedly treated to an awe-inspiring spectacle. In Montreal, Boston, Chicago, Toronto, New York, or Detroit, the fans were carried by an irresistible current that sent shivers down their spines.

Of course, the *Habitants* were not all of French Canadian origin, but they did form a compact nucleus whose team spirit, daring but well-prepared tactics, and imaginative playing style provoked their rivals' admiration and envy. In all the NHL cities, they were the team that drew the biggest crowds. When they played on the road, they were more than just the team to beat: they were a star attraction in themselves. For five years, from autumn 1955 to spring 1960, they outclassed their opponents by winning four League championships, and – above all – five Stanley Cups in a row. In only one of these seasons did they lose more than 20 games: in 1956-1957, they lost 23 out of a total of 70 regular games.

The Canadiens' publicity agent, Camil DesRoches, would often stop in front of the team pictures taken by the official Forum photographer on the day after the monumental win every spring during these years. He looked proudly at the men who were the subject of his press releases: always the same faces, on which could be seen a desire to take the *bleu-blanc-rouge* to unprecedented heights. From year to year, a new face might appear and an older player might retire, but the core remained strong and intact.

This was the team that inevitably scored goals with its two offensive lines. The first one consisted of Henri Richard, the "Pocket Rocket," flanked by his older brother Maurice on the right and Dickie Moore on the left. Opponents who managed to stave off the attack by this first lineup would be confronted by a second trio, with centre Jean Béliveau, right-winger Bernie Geoffrion, and left-winger Bert Olmstead. Both lines consisted of heavy artillery. If the adversary's offence managed to break into the Habs' zone, they would be met by Phil Goyette, Claude Provost, or André Pronovost. When the Canadiens were short-handed during penalty time, there was no match for Don Marshall on defence, even though he had played as a forward in the minors. And, depending on the season, there were also Ken Mosdell, Floyd Curry, and Marcel Bonin for the offence, as well as rookies Ralph Backstrom, Ab McDonald, and Bill Hickie.

The team's defencemen were also exceptionally strong. First and foremost, Doug Harvey, the best defenceman in the League, was paired with Tom Johnson. The second defensive line was made up of partners Bob Turner and Jean-Guy Talbot. Dollard St. Laurent completed this impenetrable brigade, followed by Albert "Junior" Langlois towards the end of that glorious reign.

Minding the net was Jacques Plante, of course – the NHL's most spectacular goaltender. In his shadow, in case Jacques was injured, was Charlie Hodge as backup goalie.

Camil DesRoches had only good things to say about the Habs. They were a group of men of a superior species – proud competitors, ready to stand up to rough play, but also capable of great finesse on skates. There was no room on the team for dead wood. The coach of *les Glorieux* was Hector "Toe" Blake, a man who often lost his temper, but one who was fundamentally fair and honest with his players. Since the days when he, Maurice Richard, and Elmer Lach had formed the offensive squad known as "the Punchline," Toe Blake had always hated to lose. Jacques had an immense respect for Blake, which dated from the years that Toe had coached the Valleyfield Braves. Blake knew what Jacques was capable of: when the tuque-sporting goalie wore the Royals uniform, he had more than once made Blake almost swallow his cigar.

In the autumn of 1955, his first year as Canadiens coach, Toe Blake made some radical changes in the team's tactics. When the puck went into the opponents' zone, he told his defencemen to stay near the enemy blueline instead of circling about in the centre zone of the rink. At first, Jacques was ill at ease with this innovation: he felt that there was too much distance between his defencemen and the net. However, it didn't take him long to get used to it. After all, it wasn't surprising that the roving goalie approved of bringing the defensive line into offensive play more often.

Besides, the defencemen themselves had had to adapt to Jacques' own characteristic style. Looking at it logically, they had to admit that he helped them regain control of the puck and move it out of their own zone more quickly. But there were also all the things the goalie said: Jacques was continually talking, commenting on the play, telling his teammates where the puck was headed. When the action heated up, he even used to tell them what they should do. However, they were never offended by it: his shouting helped to orient their game and often saved them wasted manoeuvres.

The rookies of that season, Henri Richard, Jean-Guy Talbot, and Claude Provost, were off to a promising start. Gerry McNeil hoped for a comeback, claiming that his year off had allowed him to recoup his strength and skill, but he was no longer a match for Jacques Plante and he had to settle for playing for the Royals. Charlie Hodge was sent to another Canadiens' farm team in Seattle. Jacques' position with the Habs was now unchallenged, and he justified this confidence in him by achieving two shutouts in the first two games of the season.

Jacques posted seven shutouts that season, winning his first Vézina Trophy with a goals-against average of only 1.86 per game. He was chosen for the First All-Star team, together with some of his most notable teammates: centre Jean Béliveau, the season's top scorer with 47 goals and named most useful player; right-winger Maurice Richard; and defenceman Doug Harvey, winner of the Norris Trophy.

Even more of a thrill for Jacques was being number 1 goalie of a Stanley Cup-winning team for the first time, when the Canadiens defeated the Rangers in the five-game semifinals and the Red Wings in the five-game final series.

The team was strong and seemed invincible. Toe Blake had devised an unbeatable power play. When the opponents had a man in the penalty box, Blake didn't waste any time analysing the situation. He would send Jean Béliveau onto centre ice, with Maurice Richard on his right and usually Dickie Moore, or, occasionally, Bert Olmstead on left wing. Both Harvey and Geoffrion could shoot hard and far, striking when the goaltender's view was screened by other players; if the goalie blocked one of their shots, chances were that a forward would be able to snap up the puck on the rebound and flip it into the net.

During that 1955-1956 season, the Canadiens consistently overwhelmed their opponents whenever they had the numerical advantage, often scoring two or three goals during those two minutes of penalty time. The League's executives met and decided to correct this imbalance. They wanted closer games.

A new rule came into force the following season. Rule 27(c) of the Official NHL Rules states that "if while a team is short-handed by one or more penalties the opposing team scores a goal, the first of such penalties shall automatically terminate." It was a way of limiting the damage. But it wasn't enough to slow down the Canadiens.

The team still had the wind in its sails in 1956-1957. The Habs scored the highest number of regular-season goals in the League, although the individual record that year went to Gordie Howe. The Red Wings had made an impressive comeback and were again threatening the Canadiens. The Wings' left-wing forward, Ted Lindsay, was second to Howe in the number of goals scored, and the young Detroit goalie, Glenn Hall, who had won the 1954-1955 rookie-of-the-year title, had also had a remarkable season.

Jacques Plante experienced a few health problems that kept him off the ice for most of the month of November. The medical specialists, looking for possible allergies, took a long time to determine the cause of his chronic bronchitis. However, it was the asthma that had afflicted him since childhood – the asthma that had obliged him to tend goals instead of hurtling down the ice and had driven him to knit tuques to protect himself from the cold – that became his principal adversary during these years. When Jacques was too ill to play, his replacement, Gerry McNeil, let in a whopping 32 goals in his last nine games in the National Hockey League.

In that era of hockey history, the Vézina Trophy was awarded to the goalie of the team with the least number of points given up to opponents during the regular season, not to the goaltender with the lowest individual goals-against average. Jacques' health problems and Glenn Hall's brilliance in the net had placed them on an almost equal footing, and a suspenseful competition between them went on up until the play-offs.

∞

Saturday, March 24, 1957.

It was the last game of the regular season. The Canadiens were playing the Chicago Black Hawks, who were already out of the running for a place in the semifinals. However, at the end of the season, an eliminated team would often give a hard time to a team that was on its way to a more glorious finish.

Since the beginning of the season, 155 goals had been scored against the Habs – two more than those allowed by Glenn Hall and the Red Wings. Jacques would have to achieve a shutout in this game to win the Vézina Trophy. Every goaltender always hopes that he won't let any pucks get past him, but this game was special. That same night, the Red Wings were playing against the Maple Leafs, a weak, last-place team that year. Jacques had to be invincible. The game in Toronto started at 8:00 p.m., whereas the game at the Montreal Forum was scheduled to begin half an hour later.

When Jacques skated over to his net before the beginning of the game, the scoreboard indicated that the Maple Leafs were leading by 1-0; thus, Jacques and the Canadiens were only one goal away from Glenn Hall's lead.

The tension mounted as the game went on. Jacques wasn't the only one in the St. Catherine Street hockey mecca to glance every few minutes at the scoreboard to follow what was happening in Toronto: the other players, as well as the fans, seemed as interested as he was.

Toronto scored again in the middle of the second period. Plante and Hall were now tied. But there was still a lot of time left in the Canadiens' game – an eternity for the lone soldier holding the fort. Jacques sharpened his concentration. He blocked routine shots with more than usual care. His eyes warily followed his opponents' every move: he was determined not to be caught unawares by an easy shot.

The final score of the Toronto-Detroit game flashed onto the scoreboard: Detroit had won by a score of 6-3. By allowing three goals, Hall was now trailing Jacques by one point in their race for the Vézina. And there were still nine minutes of play to go in Montreal – nine long minutes left to reduce the Chicago team to a shambles. The crowd murmured expectantly.

Unfortunately, the clock was positioned right behind Jacques' net. He couldn't see how much time remained unless he turned his head around. But how could he take his eyes off the puck, even for a second, if he was to achieve the shutout? Luckily for Jacques that night, a fan, sitting behind and to the left of the net, was aware of the goaltender's distress. He kept encouraging him, saying, "Eight minutes, Jacques... eight minutes to go. Hang in there!"

Jacques was sweating profusely. *Don't make a mistake now...don't do anything wrong...*

"Seven..."

All his muscles were tensed. If he could have caught the puck, he would have made it disappear.

"Six minutes...keep it up, Jacques!"

And Jacques kept it up.

The siren wailed to indicate the end of the game. The Habs had won, 3-0.

The fans were on their feet, applauding wildly. They were not acclaiming the win against the Hawks – not a particularly notable feat for the Habs in those days; they were acclaiming Jacques Plante, who had just posted his ninth shutout of the season and had won the Vézina Trophy for the second year in a row.

Jacques flew over the ice in his excitement. There was no time to thank the good Samaritan who had shared the countdown with him. He didn't even take the time to acknowledge the fans who, realizing the importance of the situation, had encouraged him throughout the evening. Jacques felt decidedly ill. When he reached the dressing room, he vanished into the bathroom to throw up.

∞

Pressure – the deadly pressure that can crush a man, isolate him from the people around him. There is always constant pressure on an athlete, especially one of Jacques Plante's conscientious professionalism, always striving to do better and continually under the scrutiny of very critical sports fans. The fans at the Montreal Forum were demanding: they had seen so many champions play that they expected much more from their team than the fans in other hockey cities did.

Thus, in spite of his huge success, Jacques' frequent roving beyond the goal crease was still provoking comment. During Jacques' debut in the National League, Dick Irvin's face invariably fell whenever he saw his new goaltender leave the net. Toe Blake, especially in the first two seasons as Canadiens coach, reacted the same way. How many times did Jacques have to justify his technique in the dressing room after a game? It was a good thing that he liked to talk! The sportswriters knew by now that he was a mine of information and they always lent an attentive ear.

"I prepare my sorties ahead of time," Jacques said. "When an opponent is chasing a puck that's coming into our zone, I estimate the player's speed against the puck's speed. I have to calculate it exactly right before I come out of the net, to be sure to get to the puck first and be back in the net before the other team gets control of it again. The blue-line is my guide: if the adversary hasn't crossed the blue-line yet, I can go out. Otherwise, I stay in the net."

Although Toe Blake broke into a cold sweat every time Jacques executed this manoeuvre, he was forced to recognize its effectiveness. He and the other members of the team began to notice that whenever their number 1 goalie was absent, there was a drop in the team's morale. The Canadiens had gotten used to Jacques helping them out by leaving his net to retrieve the puck and pass it to them: it made the defencemen's job that much easier.

Besides, the results spoke for themselves. In two years, Jacques had only been outplayed once in that situation, and, on the positive side, he had relaunched countless attacks for the Habs. Nonetheless, opposition to an individual who defies tradition is a common human trait, and certain fans at the Forum would start to boo whenever Jacques made the tiniest error. In an interview, he stated that he was much too involved in the game to notice them, but in fact, this was not absolutely true. When his wife attended his games, she knew very well that the hooting and booing touched a raw nerve in Jacques. She also noticed that it only came from a specific contingent of spectators – small comfort to a man who wanted his work and his judgment to be appreciated. However, it was all part of the game. A few catcalls wouldn't stop him from realizing his ambitions by playing in the way he thought best.

His teammates viewed Jacques as a "different kind of guy." How many hockey players would sit knitting or reading a biography on the train instead of joining in the everlasting card games? There was only Jean Béliveau with whom Jacques could talk about books from time to time. After a game, when the players went out to a bar, they would draw lots to see who would pay for the first round of beer. Jacques never took part in this game. "I'll pay for my own beer," he would declare.

He was always the first to return to the hotel when the Habs were on the road. He slept a lot. It was one way of controlling his asthma and bronchitis, either of which could creep up on him at any moment. However, it earned him a reputation as a loner and a skinflint.

But where sports were concerned, Jacques was never stingy with his time. He volunteered for a variety of charitable causes. In the summer, he promoted Little League baseball by acting as umpire for Pee-wee games in the Laval neighbourhood where he lived with his family. Jacques excelled at golf and soccer. He was also an excellent bowler and was often the guest of honour when new lanes were inaugurated. But baseball remained his favourite warm-weather sport.

During the summer of 1957, for example, he played first base for the St. Laurent team and won the batting title of the Quebec Senior Baseball League, with an average of .425. He knew that he attracted crowds to the games. People were coming to see the Habs' goaltender in action, but Jacques was there simply because he loved to play.

∞

There has always been a voluminous amount written about sports. From time immemorial, newspapers have dedicated miles of column space to athletes, their performances – and their opinions. The sports world is the source of hundreds of clichés and gems of journalistic wisdom.

"It's hard to reach first place, but it's even harder to stay there," is a choice example of the hackneyed phrases that abound in the sports milieu. However, like many of these sayings, it rests on a basis of truth – and it applies to a member of the glorious Canadiens Hockey Club as much as it does to the champion of an obscure bowling league.

The 1957-1958 hockey season, which ended by the Habs winning their third consecutive Stanley Cup, was strewn with obstacles.

As the season progressed, Toe Blake watched helplessly as his star players came down with injuries. The Rocket, with an injured Achilles' tendon, only played 28 of the regular season games. Bernie Geoffrion suffered a perforated intestine during a practice; the last rites were administered before he went into emergency surgery, then, after the operation, the doctors' opinion was that he would never skate again. Boom Boom overcame the dire prognosis, coming back to play just before the finals; he participated in 42 games, after all, in that unlucky season. Dickie Moore played for the last five weeks of the regular season with his right hand in a cast, which didn't prevent him from winning the scoring championship that year – an exploit that he repeated the subsequent season.

All of these unexpected pitfalls gave Toe Blake stomach ulcers, and his star goaltender did nothing to relieve them. Jacques' asthma was becoming increasingly unmanageable. He was subject to more frequent and more acute attacks that left him weakened. Also, with only a few weeks left in the regular season, he was knocked hard by Vic Staziuk of the Bruins; he suffered a concussion and was off the ice for three games.

In spite of these mishaps, the Habs showed exemplary courage and tenacity in 1957-58. They never gave up, and in the spring, they managed to finish on top in the standings, 19 points ahead of the New York Rangers. They defeated Detroit in four consecutive wins in the semifinals, to take on the Bruins in the finals. With a powerful offence, and inspired by the remarkable performance of goaltender Don Simmons, the Bostonians gave the Habs a series to remember.

∞

April 20, 1958. The Boston Garden.

The Habs were leading the Bruins three games to two. Rocket Richard had brought the fans to their feet when he scored the winning goal during overtime in the fifth game. The Canadiens were primed for action. They wanted to end the series that night if they could.

Jacques Plante in particular fervently hoped that the series would be over after the sixth game: he knew he wouldn't be able to play a seventh one. For the preceding few days, he had felt like a limp rag. He was ill – with chronic bronchitis, according to the newspapers. As if his profession were not exhausting enough in itself, Jacques' asthma was sapping all of his reserve energy. In his hotel room, he had trouble falling asleep. He was coughing, barely able to breathe. When he looked at himself in the bathroom mirror, he had the impression that he was looking at a zombie animated by a raging fever. But he was determined to play anyway. Something was pushing him to believe that if he could just drag himself that one step further, he would be able to rest on the far side of the mountain peak. The team was too close to reaching its goal; it had overcome so many problems and worked so hard to get that far. He couldn't let his teammates down at the critical moment.

That afternoon, the Canadiens had gone to see *The Bridge on the River Kwai*, a film extolling bravery and team spirit; Jacques felt that he must follow this example and persevere against all odds.

The game started. The Canadiens were in control of the puck from the beginning of the first period. Geoffrion scored a goal at 46 seconds, then The Rocket sunk his eleventh goal of the playoffs a minute later. But the Bruins were not intimidated: they clawed their way back in a relentless attack. Jacques had to block 13 shots before the period ended. Sheer adrenaline kept him alert. Miraculously, he kept his team in the game, allowing only one goal by Don McKenney.

In the second period, the Canadiens increased their lead: Béliveau scored on a spectacular assist by Geoffrion and Harvey, then Boom Boom scored his second goal of the game.

Between periods, the Habs whistled the theme from *The Bridge on the River Kwai...we've got to keep up the good work...we've got to finish it today*. Every time Jacques tried to exhale, the air was trapped in his bronchial tubes. The sound of his hoarse gasps was muffled by the fans' whistles and shouts.

In the third period, the Bruins were back on the attack. Norm Johnson scored a goal, then Larry Regan. But Jacques succeeded in putting those goals out of his mind and made a succession of impressive saves, throwing himself onto a rebounding puck, and blocking a hard, fast shot. Every time, it was harder for him to get up again. He was dizzy and struggled to get his wind back. He made a monumental effort to concentrate on the puck. He refused to give in; he was like a battered boxer who stays on his feet by sheer instinct.

In the last minute of play, with the Canadiens leading by one point, Don Simmons left his net, and a sixth Bruin attacker skated onto the ice. Jacques fended off the power play with incredible acrobatic skill, until Doug Harvey clinched the Habs' third consecutive Stanley Cup by shooting into Boston's empty cage. Jacques Plante collapsed onto the ice. His strength gone, he wept like a baby. He had called up a hidden force from deep within himself.

Camil DesRoches and physiotherapist Bill Head had to take Jacques under both arms to lead him to the dressing room. Jacques was still gasping for air – but he had held on until the end, and his team had triumphed.

∽

That year, Jacques was the victim of an injustice: he was chosen for the second rather than the first All-Star team by the panel of hockey-circuit reporters. Glenn Hall was voted in for the first-choice lineup for the second year in a row, although his goals-against average was 2.88, compared to Jacques' 2.11 – besides the fact that Hall's team had not even made it to the playoffs that season.

Jacques, like several of his teammates, had lost out precisely because of their team's superior strength. Since the Canadiens had reaped the juiciest plums of the season by winning the Stanley Cup and top points in the standings, the unspoken agreement was that the players of the other, less illustrious teams should be given individual recognition. Thus, during the five years that the Canadiens lopsidedly dominated the NHL, the Hart Trophy for most valuable player was only awarded to a Canadien once, when Jean Béliveau won it in 1955-1956. The following years, the sportswriters and analysts voted three times for Gordie Howe, and once for Andy Bathgate, for the Hart. The rookie-of-the-year title was given to a Montreal player only once during this period – to Ralph Backstrom in 1958-1959 – and none of the Habs were awarded the Lady Byng Trophy for the season's most courteous player during these years. Only the Norris Trophy for best defensive player seemed to belong in perpetuity to Doug Harvey, who won it every year from 1955 to 1966, with the exception of 1959, when it went to another Canadiens defenceman, Tom Johnson.

The awarding of the Vézina Trophy for best goaltender, on the other hand, was based on statistics rather than on a vote by a panel of sportswriters. The following season (1958-1959), Jacques won the Vézina for the fourth time, and was finally chosen to play on the first All-Star team. That year, the Canadiens won both the League championship and the Stanley Cup – for the fourth consecutive time.

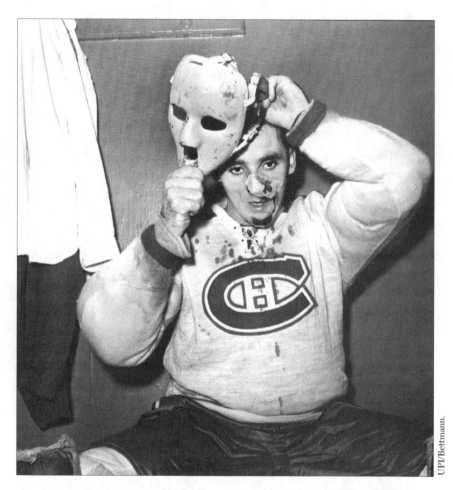

In New York City on November 1, 1959, after a facial injury,
Jacques Plante wears a mask for the first time in a regular game.

7

The Phantom Puck-Stopper

November 1, 1959.

The noisy fans who crowded into Madison Square
Garden in New York City didn't realize that they
were attending a historic game. They were there
because they loved sports, because New York was the
show capital of North America, and hockey, being the
fastest and most suspenseful sport around, gave them
great entertainment value. They flocked to the
Garden in droves, even though they knew that their
home team was not on a par with the Montreal
Canadiens.

The Rangers were in fifth place in the NHL
standings, barely ahead of the Black Hawks, with

whom they disputed the honour of being the most lacklustre team in the NHL that season. There was only one Ranger who qualified as a star: the remarkably talented Andy Bathgate, who had finished the last two seasons as one of the five top scorers in the League. His 1958-1959 goal count had been 30. But the Rangers didn't have much hope of defeating the Habs that evening, especially as the *bleu-blanc-rouge* was on a seven-game winning streak.

Three minutes into the game, the kind of incident that marks a turning point in a goalkeeper's life occurred in the midst of a scramble for the puck in front of the Canadiens net. Bent almost double, Jacques vainly tried to spot the puck. Andy Bathgate was waiting for a pass, five metres away from the net. When he did have the opportunity to shoot, he slammed a powerful backhand shot right into Jacques' face.

Jacques immediately collapsed onto the ice, bleeding heavily. The puck had hit him on the left side of his face, alongside his nose. In an instant, the team physician, Hector Dubois, arrived to help. Jacques gradually came to his senses and rose to his feet. Supported by Maurice Richard and Dickie Moore, he made his way off the ice. Holding a towel to his face, he walked to the first-aid room. He was given seven stitches to sew up the cut that ran down to his upper lip.

In those days, every hockey team had only one goaltender in uniform, and was given twenty minutes to get their netminder back into shape to continue the game. Clearly worried, Toe Blake came to talk to Jacques as he lay on the medical room table. When

Jacques saw him, he immediately said, "I want to play with my mask on."

Blake grimaced; however, he rarely lost his cool without a good reason. "We'll see, we'll see," he murmured.

With his long experience in competitive sports, Blake decided to use the full twenty minutes that was allotted to Jacques to determine whether he could recover sufficiently to go back on the ice.

In the corridor outside, Blake saw the Rangers' general manager, Murray "Muzz" Patrick, and asked, "Do you have a backup goaltender available?"

"We have two," answered Patrick. "There's Arnie Knox. He's thirty-three years old. He used to play in the city league and he practises with us sometimes. He works as an usher here. Do you want to see him?"

Blake shook his head. "And the other one?"

Muzz Patrick grinned. "A junior, Joe Shaeffer, but he hasn't been on skates yet this season."

Toe Blake tilted back his trademark fedora and scratched his head. He wanted more time to think. He didn't need anyone to draw a picture for him: with an amateur in the nets, that would be the end of the Habs' beautiful streak. He hated the thought of handing the opponents a win without a fight.

Jacques opened his swollen lips with difficulty and said tersely: "I won't go back into the game without the mask."

Blake realized full well that he would be creating a precedent, but in the circumstances, he had no choice. He shrugged his shoulders and snarled, "All right, Jacques, you can wear it this time if you want."

The coach was still ruminating over the problem when Jacques got up and unsteadily crossed the ice to the visitors' dressing room. He had miraculously resuscitated. The fans gave him a thunderous ovation while the organ played "For He's a Jolly Good Fellow."

A few minutes later, with a bandage covering his wound and his sweater still stained with blood, Jacques Plante donned his protective mask for the remainder of the game. No, he hadn't got the day mixed up with Halloween: he knew perfectly well where he was and what he was doing. Thus, the fans in Madison Square Garden that night were treated to the sight of a masked phantom appearing on the ice: it was the first time that a goaltender wore a mask in the modern version of the game of hockey.

The mask: for the past two years, Jacques Plante had been its most ardent defender. For two years, he had tried to convince the hockey brass of the absolute necessity of wearing it in a sport that was getting faster every year. That evening at Madison Square Garden, in the most populous city in the NHL, Jacques had an all-important point to make. With his critics ready to pounce on him, he had to show, beyond any doubt or argument, that wearing the facemask did not take anything away from a goaltender's performance – that, on the contrary, wearing it could only improve a goalie's skill by giving him more confidence to practise his art.

∞

The mask. The subject was continually rehashed on radio and television, kindling a mounting interest in it.

People remembered that Gerry McNeil had ended his career prematurely because his fear of injury had made him too nervous during games. Terry Sawchuk of the Bruins had stopped playing in mid-season that year, claiming that he was "eating much too much rubber." The mask: it all came back down to the mask.

Goaltending has always been the most dangerous position in hockey, but just a few years before, there were only one or two players per team who had mastered the art of the slapshot. In a short interval, the quantity of these deadly shots had multiplied and the chances of a goalie being injured had sharply increased. Young forwards like Bobby Hull could fire shots that reached a speed over 160 kilometres an hour. Even if the goaltender was not hit directly by one of these zingers, a ricochet could be almost as dangerous. One can imagine the impact of a puck travelling at 175 kilometres an hour hitting a goalie's bare face.

Before he wore the mask for the first time in regular season play on that first of November, Jacques himself had received more than two hundred stitches to his face. His nose had been broken four times; his cheekbones and jawbones had also been fractured. Several of these injuries had been inflicted by teammates during practices. In 1954, a shot by Habs left-winger Bert Olmstead had shattered Jacques' cheekbone and had kept him off the ice for five weeks. The year after that, his left cheekbone and his nose were fractured by a shot by teammate Don Marshall, deflected by the massive Butch Bouchard.

A thoughtful fan had sent Jacques, anonymously, a protective plastic mask that covered his face from forehead to chin. Jacques had begun using it regularly during practices, even though his range of vision was not a hundred percent complete. During one session, he had foregone the mask and had received a puck between the eyes; after that, he had worn it unfailingly during practices. It had become accepted to wear this additional protection during practice sessions, but not in the games.

On top of having to prove his point to his coach, Jacques' innovative gesture had brought him a hail of criticism from other sources. Several opponents of the use of protective headgear were outspoken in belittling him – of course, almost none of them had ever had to stand between the goal posts while being exposed to shots by well-trained athletes at the peak of their form. Jacques ran the gamut of remarks of all kinds. The typical criticism reflected the entrenched attitudes of die-hard conservatives. Rationalizations abounded, for example:

"It gets too hot under the mask and the sweat runs into the goalie's eyes."

"The visibility isn't good enough: Plante can't see when the puck is near his feet."

"The mask is too heavy: it strains his neck muscles and makes his head move more slowly."

A few of the comments were valid. Jacques himself had acknowledged that the masks he had worn during practice sessions weren't perfect. However, a few of the hockey pundits used more puerile excuses for banning the mask from regular games.

"The goaltenders in our club will never wear a mask," pronounced Muzz Patrick of the Rangers, "because female hockey fans like to see the players' faces!"

Another type of comment reflected a macho attitude in sports: "A real man wouldn't hide his face from the opponents."

Some coaches, including Toe Blake, thought that if a goaltender wore a mask all the time, he would feel overconfident and this might diminish his concentration. It would be easier to outplay a goalie who had lost that extra alertness brought on by fear, which kept him on his guard at all times. This was an argument that weighed more than the others. Whenever someone would ask him about the mask, Blake would chaw on his cigar with a sour expression on his face – he was especially sensitive to the controversy because it had been Jacques, his own goalie, who had provoked it.

This was why Blake had been so reluctant to give in to Jacques on that November evening in New York. Grumbling as he tilted his fedora even further back on his head, he knew that he had not heard the last of the matter.

If, that first time, the Rangers had gone on to score five or six goals, Blake would have used all his powers of persuasion to prohibit the use of the face-mask. However, in spite of an injury that might have turned the game into a rout for the Canadiens, things turned out quite differently.

∞

The masked man in the bloodstained uniform took his position in the goal mouth. Not only was he determined to protect his team's net with his usual skill, but he also had something to prove. He no longer accepted that his duty as goaltender included the risk of being blinded or disfigured.

Jacques made several saves as soon as the shots started coming at him. His teammates, gaining confidence, went all out to sway the odds in the Canadiens' favour. Dickie Moore scored his fourth goal of the season on a rebound from a shot by The Rocket. André Pronovost marked the second goal for the Habs by flipping the puck into the corner of the net on his own rebound. Finally, Bernie Geoffrion scored his seventh of the season, outplaying Lorne "Gump" Worsley with a pass from behind the net that bounced off John Hanna's skate into the net.

In the third period, the beefy Rangers goaltender managed to block shots by all four Canadiens who broke away from the defence to take unimpeded shots on him. Jacques remained solid as the match wore on. Rangers fans had to wait until the middle of the third period when Camille Henry, a terror near the net, caught the rebound from a slapshot by Andy Bathgate and sent it over Jacques Plante, who was stretched out on the ice.

The final score: Canadiens 3, Rangers 1. Jacques was mobbed by his teammates. Toe Blake was the first to congratulate him for his brilliant feat, and the Habs continued on the road to glory. The mask had entered the game of hockey once and for all.

∞

Of course, winning a battle did not mean the war was over. But after that first game, Jacques had complete confidence in his mask. He knew that it was efficacious and essential. Besides, since he had first tried the prototype during practices, the product had been refined and perfected. The improved version was now made of fibreglass instead of the original plastic.

This latest technological improvement to the piece of protective equipment was the work of another hockey fan. Bill Burchmore was head of sales and promotion at the Montreal branch of Fiberglas Canada Ltd. He was crazy about hockey and was an unconditional Habs man. He had been a goaltender, then a forward, and eventually became a coach, teaching hockey basics to kids between the ages of eight and ten. One of his protégés had became a professional and was on Jacques Plante's team: none other than Dickie "Digger" Moore.

Burchmore had attended a 1958 playoff game between Montreal and Boston, during which the puck had hit Jacques in the face. He had immediately written to Jacques, telling him that he had been working on a concept for an original mask and was now ready to develop the product. He knew, from his own experience, that for a goalie to accept wearing a mask, it had to have three essential characteristics: it had to be light, it had to be unbreakable, and it had to press close against the face to allow for maximum peripheral vision. Burchmore came up with the concept of a fibreglass mask. This new material, which had not yet been fully exploited, seemed to fit the bill: it was strong, light, and, most importantly, it was easily moulded.

Jacques had found the idea interesting, but at the time, he was still doubtful about the material's effectiveness. He waited a year before agreeing to lend himself to Burchmore's experiment. It was only in the summer of 1959 that Jacques went to the Montreal General Hospital, encouraged by the Canadiens' physician, Dr. Ian Milne, and the team physiotherapist, Bill Head. Under Dr. Milne's supervision, a mould of Jacques' face was taken.

Bill Burchmore got to work. His first effort was a fibreglass mask baked in an oven and saturated with polyester resin. Rubber strips lined the inside to absorb any shocks to the forehead, cheekbones, and jaw. The final product was only three millimetres thick, but was as resistant as steel.

Jacques tried it out during the next practice session and found that it fulfilled its purpose perfectly. However, his coach was still not convinced: making changes when things were going well had never been his style.

"It's not a bad idea, Jacques," Toe Blake told him. "But I'd advise you to use it only during practices. If you start the season wearing a mask and you let in a few shots that looked easy to stop, the fans are going to hassle you and blame the mask."

Jacques had accepted this reasoning, which was precisely why he had not been wearing the mask on November 1st. But that night, he could no longer hold himself back – just as he couldn't suppress the business instinct that lurked inside him. As soon as he saw how well the mask worked, he went into partnership with Burchmore to be the exclusive makers of it. No manufacturer could have believed more in a product than Jacques Plante did: he was staking his professional reputation on it.

∞

It always takes an amazing amount of stubborn courage to change the prevailing customs in professional sports. It took a large dose of conviction and exceptional strength of character to wear a mask in pro hockey, when only one other player in the NHL – Charlie Burns, an American player for the Detroit Red Wings – had worn a helmet during games, making him look like an extraterrestrial in the eyes of the fans and the other players. Jacques had to face a barrage of taunts. People said that he looked like a ghost and that he should paint the mask that must have come straight out of a Hollywood horror flick. This was unfair: it was only later that film directors created monsters who looked like they were wearing hockey masks!

Jacques continued to wear the mask amidst the slurs and ridicule; in any case, he was playing so well that no one could justifiably reproach him for it. The Canadiens chalked up 11 wins in a row, fought 18 games without a defeat, finished in first place in the League standings, and won the Stanley Cup in only 8 playoff games – with 4 wins over the Black Hawks, who had the season's scoring champion, Bobby Hull, on the team. Jacques even posted two shutouts in the semi-finals against the Hawks before giving the Habs 4 wins against Toronto in the finals. The verdict on Jacques' performance during the series: terrific! Three shutouts, and an unimaginably low goals-against average of 1.38! No hockey goaltender had ever achieved such a record.

The protective mask remained a hot topic among hockey commentators and fans, but they gave a more positive slant. Jacques had succeeded in shutting the critics' mouths. League president Clarence Campbell even stated, "Sending a man into the nets without a mask is the equivalent of sending him to the gallows!"

The Canadiens brought home their fifth Stanley Cup in a row – another record – while Jacques Plante, the masked goaltender, wrote another page of hockey history by winning his fifth Vézina Trophy in five years, all of which was satisfactorily conclusive.

Montrealers became accustomed to lining up on St. Catherine Street in April, on one of the first warm days of the year, to acclaim their heroes who rode down the street in luxury convertibles. Canadiens fans, while never tiring of the taste of victory, began to feel that the famous Stanley Cup parade was a permanent feature of their lives.

8

On Top, and Back Down Again

It all seemed too easy. With the victories and honours piling up, there was the danger of acquiring the illusion of invincibility. From his debut in the NHL until the 1960-1961 season, Jacques had accumulated the best results of any goaltender in National League history. Only Terry Sawchuk had maintained a lower goals-against average after six complete seasons of play, and only Bill Durnan had won five Vézina trophies within six years. But neither Durnan nor Vézina had played so often on a team of Stanley Cup winners. The trophies, titles, and records all clearly showed that Jacques Plante was a champion.

But what Jacques had accomplished in his career went beyond the statistics: in six years, he had radically

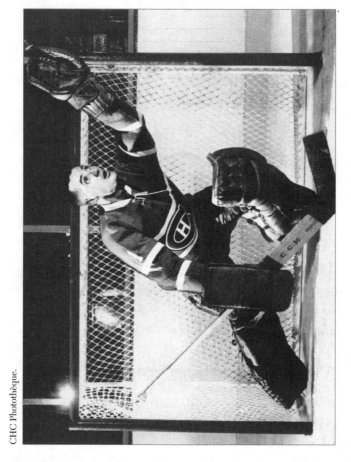

Jacques Plante created a new goaltending style that the fans adored.

transformed the art of hockey goaltending. He had introduced a highly individual new style and gained acceptance for it, to the extent that his counterparts on other teams had begun to imitate him. More importantly, he had initiated a different way of practising and of viewing the profession.

Like anyone who carries out a revolution in their field, Jacques had his detractors, vehement naysayers who refused to admit that the game of hockey could be changing right under their noses – the kind of people who always look for the negative side of any innovation, and worse, who enviously try to put down anyone who might be getting "too big for their boots." When they can't support their arguments by concrete facts, they search for personal weaknesses to criticize. These gripers never stand as an identifiable group against which it is possible to defend oneself. They make sporadic forays into the public eye, changing their faces and adding their venomous innuendos to the ebb and flow of rumours – rumours that are discredited when you're on top, but re-emerge when you slip up. And if Jacques Plante the goaltender possessed undeniably remarkable qualities, Jacques Plante the man was, of course, human, with human foibles, and it was not in his nature to hide them. A solitary bastion against the pucks, he was a public figure who never missed a chance to say what was on his mind.

Jacques was considered to have a big mouth, which was good in some circumstances and bad in others. On the ice, he sent out a continual stream of comments and instructions, directing and encouraging his teammates. From his position, he had a good view of the whole game, and as he didn't have to be on the lookout for bodychecks all the time, he could follow the action with closer attention than the other players could.

A big mouth!...just because he liked to analyse all aspects of the game and was never afraid to express his opinion. Jacques was the most articulate hockey player of his generation. It was undoubtedly his perfectionism that made him the butt of criticism from this time onward. He loved the sport passionately. He lived hockey during all his waking hours and probably even in his sleep, not only because of his desire to excel – the ultimate goal of champions – but also because he wanted to stay actively aware of all the facets of the game. When he returned home or to his hotel room after a match, he ran through all three periods in his mind, like a film reel. With his remarkable memory and powers of concentration, he would relive every goal scored by the opponents, seeking out the error to be corrected – the weak point to overcome, the trap to avoid – any detail he could change to become even better.

In the dressing room, or on the train that brought the players home to Montreal after a game away, reporters liked to solicit Jacques' opinion on a particular play, or on a goal that he may have given away in a moment of weakness or distraction. Observant analyst that he was, Jacques would often point out some of his teammates' errors in his answers. Naturally, this rubbed some of the players the wrong way. None of them liked having their mistakes mentioned out loud, especially by a member of their own team when talking to newspaper reporters! But this was Jacques' irremediable habit, mainly because he adored to discuss hockey. Whenever a reporter asked him a question, he would immediately launch into a detailed and accurate explanation, pinpointing the exact time and place that an error had occurred, whether due to negligence at centre ice or to a lack of alertness on the part of the defence. Always fair, Jacques would candidly admit to his own errors and lack of judgment. Later, he became an excellent hockey analyst in his occasional newspaper columns. He enjoyed writing and did it well. His verbal comments, however, which inevitably appeared in the next morning's newspapers, often backfired, particularly when he was misquoted. This happened often, since the reporters were usually in a rush to hand in their copy before their deadline. Misunderstandings would occur, and some of his teammates grumbled that Jacques wrongly blamed them for goals that he let in.

No matter what the circumstance, Jacques never hesitated to say what was on his mind. He openly displayed his peculiar forthright brand of professionalism and his demanding passion for the game. The inevitable negative reactions added to the pressure that he already faced as a goaltender. Jacques Plante had many friends and admirers, but he also had enemies.

In the world of sports, everything is relative: an enormous amount of discussion goes on. There are more armchair analysts than athletes. Thus, in the early 1960s, the sportswriters of all the dailies tossed the question back and forth in their columns: who was the best goaltender in the NHL? Jacques Plante's style was compared to that of Terry Sawchuk, and to that of the young Glenn Hall – although both these goalies had been largely inspired by Jacques' innovations. Sawchuk himself declared that, in his opinion, Jacques was the world's best goalkeeper. In spite of this, negative comments still came in:

"If he didn't have Harvey in front of him..."

"If the Canadiens weren't such a strong team..."

"He doesn't have to stop as many pucks as the other goalies."

Or, in defense of Jacques Plante, it was said, "Yes, but it's harder to block shots when you only have a few coming at you: your concentration suffers."

And, in the headlines of a major daily newspaper: "Jacques Plante is the key to the Canadiens' success."

Dickie Moore declared: "No team could win the Stanley Cup, let alone win it many times over without an excellent goaltender. And we have the best."

In any event, Jacques' absences never went unnoticed. The Habs just weren't the same without him in the nets. And in spite of his nagging respiratory problems, Jacques did the impossible by playing in all the games. Champions must show their courage and unshakable resolve.

∽

The 1960-1961 NHL season was marked by the departure of a legend: Maurice Richard, injured too often during the previous seasons, realized that his performance was flagging. It wasn't advisable to ask a star to stay on as an ordinary player – not a star of The Rocket's stature.

It was also the season when the slapshot came into its own. Bobby Hull, the blond comet of the Chicago

Black Hawks, commanded the hardest and fastest slap-shot in pro hockey. The fastest skater in the NHL, Hull could attain a speed of 50 kilometres an hour after just a few strides. A puck shot by a player going that fast would streak towards the net at 170 kilometres an hour, and a backhand shot, at 155 kilometres an hour. Even a back-hander by Bobby Hull was stronger than a slapshot by any of the other forwards in the League.

Not all of the goaltenders in the League had adopted the mask as standard protection as yet, but even the last holdouts were seriously considering it. Jacques Plante expressed it eloquently for all of them: "A goaltender shouldn't even blink when Hull sends up a slapshot. In the fraction of a second, you can lose sight of the puck and let in a goal, or get hit by the puck. Even if your leg pads are thick, you still feel the impact. And if you get hit on the arm or even on the fingers, you feel an electric shock that puts your arm out of service for a few minutes."

That season, more and more players took their cue from Bobby Hull. Although they didn't all achieve the same results as the Black Hawks whiz, slapshots became the norm in NHL games, with the puck travel-ling at much higher speeds than in the past. Added to this was the fact that hockey sticks were designed with thinner, curved blades; this modified the puck's trajec-tory when a player fired off a shot. That year, the total number of goals scored in the League rose sharply – by 232 points! Not surprisingly, the Black Hawks won the Stanley Cup, spearheaded by Bobby Hull.

It was Jacques' most difficult year since joining the big league.

∞

In the very first games of that season, he realized that he had a worrisome problem in his left knee. When he least expected it, he would feel an excruciating pain. It would mysteriously cease, then return a few days later.

He acknowledged that the pain was there, but he couldn't understand how or when he might have injured the knee. Perhaps he had been hit without realizing it. Perhaps a player had fallen on the knee during a fast and furious goal-mouth scrum, and he hadn't noticed the effects right away. Jacques just couldn't remember.

The pain got progressively worse. He began to feel it every time he made a lateral slide or executed a rapid block with his leg. Sometimes it was unbearable. He knew that it was making him less agile on the ice: by trying to protect his left knee, he would falter slightly in making the appropriate blocks with his leg pads. This chink in his armour affected all the interrelated movements of his performance and took the edge off his reflexes. To try to compensate for this weak point, Jacques would make the first move when an opponent was coming towards the net. It was the most foolhardy thing that a goaltender in the big league could do: shots by the best forwards were simply too fast and too accurate.

When Jacques had X-rays taken at the hospital, no abnormality was detected. But he was still experiencing severe pain. What bothered him most of all was the idea that the fans, and soon, the team management, would start to think that the problem was not in his knee, but in his head. Rumours began to circulate that besides his chronic asthma, Jacques Plante was suffering from other problems – psychosomatic ones.

Finally, Jacques appealed to his coach: "I can't go on like this, *cercueil!* What can I do to get rid of it?"

Toe Blake had seen a lot of hockey. He had known many athletes at their peak and had seen more than one of them struggling against an unaccountable, episodic slump. He had never been a goalie himself, but he offered a tentative answer: "Bill Durnan's decline started when he was sliding onto the ice too much. The more often he slid, the longer it took him to get up again."

"What should I do, then?"

"Try staying on your feet as much as you can. During the practice sessions, don't slide onto the ice, even if your net fills with pucks. During the games, try some other moves as well. Then you'll be able to get up faster when you do have to slide."

Another time, Jacques confessed to Blake that he was having difficulty responding to backhand shots. The coach immediately re-organized the practice sessions to include more backhands, without telling his players that the exercise was mainly for Jacques' benefit. However, in the end, Blake came back to the same old argument: "It's the mask, Jacques. It makes you feel too sure of yourself."

But in this matter, Jacques stood firm. "If I have to take off my mask, I'll hang up my skates."

It had taken Jacques so long to convince the hockey world of the importance of the protective headgear that he wasn't willing to give up at the first sign of a problem. But he did agree to undergo a series of visual tests at the Montreal General Hospital. Jacques was tested for the speed at which he could identify colours of different intensities projected at different angles – first with his mask on, and again without the mask.

When the session ended, the results were not divulged immediately. A few days later, Jacques was relieved to learn – from the newspapers – that his mask had nothing to do with any imperfections in his performance.

Nevertheless, he was willing to admit that things were not going well for him in the net. He was letting in goals of a type that he had never allowed before. As the season wore on, he looked less and less like the extraordinary goalkeeper of the previous five years. It was obvious that he lacked confidence, and it seemed that he had lost his usual deftness and the fine sense of timing that is crucial for excellence in goaltending. And finally, he regularly complained of knee pain.

The armchair analysts rashly concluded that Jacques was becoming delusional and that it was the beginning of the end of his career. As for his complaints of pain, the least unkind of these amateur commentators said that the goaltender had found the perfect excuse for his poor performance that year. The sports world is notoriously fickle; however, this time, the statistics confirmed their impressions. In the first 21 games of the season, Jacques had already allowed 69 goals, and the Canadiens had won 10 games, lost 7, and tied 4. For a few days in November, after a bang-up collision with Dickie Moore, Jacques could barely walk.

On November 26th, Blake removed Jacques from the lineup and sent in Charlie Hodge. The little substitute played very well during Jacques' absence: of the 20 games that they played from the end of November until mid-January, with Hodge in the nets, the Habs won 15, lost 4, and tied one.

In spite of this forced rest, Jacques' condition did not improve. With less action demanded of it, his left knee seemed to be regaining its strength, but it was still fragile, and Jacques was unable to carry out his saves in his usual style.

It was the low point of that unlucky season. Rumours that Jacques Plante was about to be traded began to circulate. People were even saying that he himself had asked Frank Selke to trade him to another team.

"What? Who told you that?" Jacques asked the reporter from *Parlons Sport* during a telephone interview. "I never said that to anyone, and I would never ask such a thing. The Canadiens are the best team in the League as far as making money is concerned. Why would I change for a worse situation? A Rangers or a Bruins player might ask to be traded, but not a Canadiens player, *cercueil de cercueil!*"

"When are you coming back to play?" asked the journalist.

"How do expect me to know that? The doctors don't even know!"

But crucial weeks were passing, and the team management decided that something had to be done. In the same office where Jacques had known some of his happiest moments, Frank Selke did not mince words: "Listen, Jacques, I think you're going nowhere by letting yourself get stuck in this situation. I've got to think about the end of the season, and if, for some reason, I had to replace Charlie Hodge, what would I do? It doesn't look like you're getting any better. If you can't get all your skill back, I'm going to have to send you down."

"Send me down where?" asked Jacques apprehensively.

"To the Royals."

Jacques swallowed in consternation. Truly, calamity had struck – it really wasn't his season. After giving a consistently astounding, record-breaking performance as a goaltender, he was back where he had been nine years ago, before starting out with the Canadiens. For an instant, jumbled images flashed through his mind, of a long road of determined efforts and glory-covered achievements – all to end with this painful fall into anonymity.

Of course, Jacques could have chosen to retire at this point: there is nothing humiliating about stopping when you can no longer carry out the job, especially when you're in pain. But this thought was quickly brushed aside by a resurgence of the familiar excitement of taking on a challenge. Jacques felt that he had yet another battle to fight. His sense of honour was aroused; he didn't waste any time arguing. He lifted his head and looked straight at his employer. "When do you want me to report to the team, Mr. Selke?"

The general manager smiled at Jacques warmly. He had obviously been relieved of a heavy burden. "That's exactly what I expected you to say, Jacques. You're going to play against the Sudbury Wolves tomorrow night," he said.

The Royals were limping along in last place in the Eastern Professional League standings, but Jacques couldn't have cared less. For the first time in years, he didn't have to aim for a championship or a trophy. He could measure himself by his own standards. His only ambition was to work hard to recover his strength and to play with all of his old skill – to become Jacques Plante again.

"I want to play hockey, and I want to know what I am capable of," was his answer to a reporter who was rather intimidated at interviewing a man who had been one of the best and most celebrated players in the NHL less than a year before.

And to the reporter's hint that he had fallen from grace into a rut, Jacques' reply was characteristically proud and optimistic. "I am not at all embarrassed wearing the Royals' uniform," he said. "It's a chance for me to get back into shape, to find out if my reflexes are still good."

Another motive for sending Jacques to the Royals was that his presence would boost attendance for Floyd Curry's team, which was only attracting an average of 2,000 fans per game, due to its poor showing. The Royals' general manager, Frank Carlin, counted on Jacques to bring that number up to 5000. Even if Jacques might not be able to take the team to the finals, at least he would save it from a heavy financial loss.

It turned out that Jacques' stint in the minor league lasted only three weeks. His average with the Royals was 3 goals-against, but he made up for it by his showmanship and crowd appeal – skating far from the net, advising his defencemen and stopping opponents on breakaways before they could get near the net. In fact, Jacques was playing so well that Frank Selke revised his opinion and got in touch with him.

Although Charlie Hodge had given an excellent account of himself during the time that he replaced Jacques, he was less confident in the nets than Jacques was. His teammates had adjusted their play in consequence by concentrating more on defence, and the Habs' results reflected this. Although the situation wasn't catastrophic by any means, the Canadiens were in second place in the League standings, behind the Maple Leafs. Players on opposing teams were becoming familiar with the new goalie's technique, and some of them had figured out how to outplay him. Hodge seemed less alert and was starting to allow goals more frequently.

It was time for a reassessment of the situation. Selke arranged a meeting with Toe Blake, Bill Head, and Jacques.

"We want to get back into first place," said Selke. "I think we need Jacques' experience and fighting spirit."

Toe Blake was skeptical and glanced at Jacques, whose knee was taped up.

"Give it to us straight, Jacques – how do you feel?"

Jacques didn't hesitate for a second: he decided to be perfectly honest.

"I feel about seventy-five per cent of my capacity."

Blake was worried and went into a confidential huddle with Bill Head to discuss the goalie's condition in greater detail. A few minutes later, the team physiotherapist came over to Jacques and took him aside. "They want to hear you say that you're a hundred per cent fit. You know that a goalie's most important quality is self-confidence," he confided.

Jacques shook his head and replied, "I can't tell them I'm a hundred per cent when it's actually only seventy-five. But I think that seventy-five per cent isn't too bad, considering the circumstances. And I should add that Jacques Plante at seventy-five per cent of his capacity is as good as any other goalie in the NHL."

Bill Head grinned.

"I think that's the answer they'd like to hear."

They did like it, and Jacques went back onto the ice for the Canadiens. The gamble paid off: Jacques allowed 43 goals in the last 19 games of the regular season, maintaining a goals-against average of 2.26, and the Habs reached the finish line ahead of the Leafs.

That year, Bernie Geoffrion was NHL scoring champ, a few points ahead of second-place Jean Béliveau. He also won the Hart Trophy, and most importantly, duplicated Maurice Richard's fabulous record of 50 goals in a season. However, Geoffrion had played 64 games to reach the half-century mark, whereas The Rocket had accomplished this feat in only 50 games. Setting a new record, Doug Harvey won the Norris Trophy for the sixth time.

The Habs were shaken by the Black Hawks' power when they met their adversaries in the first round of the post-season playoffs. The Chicago goalie, Glenn Hall, achieved two shutouts, in the fifth and sixth games respectively. To play in these two last games, Jacques had to have his knee anesthetized.

Toe Blake chewed on his cigar in frustration and complained about the referees' decisions and the linesmen's calls. At the end of the last game, he finally lost control of himself, jumped onto the ice, went over to the linesman and tried to punch him. The Habs' coach was given a stiff fine for this misdemeanour.

The night the Canadiens were eliminated, their goaltender knew that he had an important decision to make. His asthma was still troubling him, and, even if the X-rays hadn't revealed the cause, his knee was hurting so much that it kept him awake at night. Jacques was exhausted. He had to choose between retirement and an operation. Perhaps the doctors would be able to discover the problem by exploratory surgery: what they couldn't see from the outside or in the X-rays, they might find by probing inside the knee. His future depended on it. Unless the gossips were right: perhaps the injury was the fruit of his imagination after all.

From any point of view, Jacques was at a turning point in his career. He wanted to know what the future held for him. Again, he decided to risk all. As curious as ever, Jacques wanted to get underneath the surface of things. He decided to undergo surgery.

∞

"Did they find out why my knee was hurting me so much?"

Jacques had hardly opened his eyes in the recovery room before asking the question that had kept him in suspense for so many months. The attending nurse smiled at him.

"Yes, they found out. Your cartilage was really messed up."

Jacques went back to sleep, relieved. By nature, he was too brave to be a hypochondriac, but even so, he had experienced some serious self-doubt.

A few hours later, when the anesthetic's effects had completely worn off, the surgeon, Dr. Shannon, informed Jacques that the cartilage in his knee had been in very bad condition, in three places. In one place, it had lost all its elasticity; another piece was crushed between two bones, where friction caused intolerable pain; and a third section of cartilage was badly torn.

"It took me fifty minutes to put everything back together again," said the surgeon. "I don't know how you managed to mind the nets with your knee in such a state."

Jacques didn't say a word. He looked over at his wife, who smiled at him. He knew that he had been freed from an enormous weight. Now that the main obstacle was out of the way, he could depend on himself to climb back up the slope. He had done that all his life, and he was used to it. He knew that he could regain his physical stamina.

The early May sun was shining through the window of the hospital room. Now, Jacques could say it out loud, and, above all, he could say it to himself, "I'm not finished, *cercueil!*"

The period of inactivity at the hospital gave Jacques a chance to think. For long hours, he was alone, forced to reassess his life. He realized that he had accomplished an incredible feat: with five Vézina

Trophies, he could retire and most likely be inducted into the Hockey Hall of Fame. It would be a source of personal satisfaction, naturally. But Jacques was aiming even higher.

The warrior suddenly shook himself. He had another challenge to face. If everything had seemed easy on the crest of the wave, all it meant was that he had to try twice as hard in the slough. At the same time, he realized what it meant to be a professional athlete, and what was expected of him: to give, always give, overcoming the suffering that, however bad it may be, brings a person maturity.

Something Frank Selke had said to him one day came back into Jacques' mind: "You'll always be better when you have something to fight for."

Now Jacques had something to fight for. He didn't just want to make a comeback; he wanted to play better than ever.

"*Cercueil!* They'll see what Jacques Plante is made of!"

Jacques designed a training program for himself, with the help of physiotherapist Bill Head, who had never doubted that Jacques' knee problems were real.

"You'll have to work very hard, Jacques. Your left knee is five centimetres less in circumference than your right. You'll have to build up your muscles."

"I'm ready," was the prompt answer.

During the summer of 1961, probably no one in the Montreal region worked harder or more tenaciously than Jacques Plante.

Propelled by his desire to surpass himself yet again, to come back with a flourish, and to overcome past failures, Jacques began exercising methodically and conscientiously. He walked on a treadmill; he made sure that his left leg was involved when lifting weights; he constantly moved his knee, to help it recover all its strength and flexibilty. While he watched television or read, he would continue exercising his left leg, bending and stretching it. Along with everyone else who was interested in sports, he followed the epic race between Mickey Mantle and Roger Maris to break Babe Ruth's record of 60 home runs in one season. All eyes were glued to the performances of the two New York Yankee teammates, including Jacques, but he never lapsed in his training. He knew that his future depended on his efforts.

He took his golf clubs out again. On the links, he had occasion to meet people, and these encounters were encouraging for him. He also took long walks. At home, he spent his free time doing carpentry, something he had always enjoyed. He did all the repairs and improvements to his eleven-room house in Laval-des-Rapides by himself, just as he had drawn up the construction plans for it years earlier.

Jacques kept up a lively interest in everything and everyone around him. Soon, he was able to run without difficulty. He refused to go easy on his left leg. He knew that the coming 1961-1962 season was crucial for him. He would have to prove that he wasn't a has-been in pro sports; he knew it, but the rest of the world did not.

Jacques was aware that the Canadiens autumn training camp would be different from usual that year. The Habs had lost their position as League champions, and some changes would certainly take place.

For one thing, competition for the position of number 1 goaltender was going to be sharper. The team had succeeded in obtaining the young Cesare Maniago from the Maple Leafs. It was obvious that the management was taking exceptional measures to avoid being left without a good netminder in the off-chance that Jacques was not up to scratch. They could count on a reliable pair of backup goalies with Maniago and Charlie Hodge.

Besides that, four Habs stalwarts had been traded to the New York Rangers: Doug Harvey, Junior Langlois, Bob Turner, and Jean-Guy Gendron. The Canadiens club was ready to do anything to put together a championship team. But Jacques Plante had to prove over again that he had a place in the kingdom of hockey.

Toe Blake was optimistic. He reminded himself (and other people) that Jacques was always at his best when the going got tough. And although several of the veterans were gone, the Habs were rejuvenated with Jean-Guy Tremblay, Jean Gauthier, Lou Fontinato at the blue-line, and the speedy winger, Gilles Tremblay, out in front.

Soon, Jacques was back in Frank Selke's office. He knew it like the back of his hand by now: it had been the scene of all his contract negotiations. This time, however, Jacques did not have the chips on his side, and had to accept a salary drop of $1000. Still, he got Selke to promise him a bonus if he played an extraordinary season. That was his main ambition, and it mattered to him more than anything else.

9

The Masked Wonder

By September, Jacques was restless. He was eager to don his heavy leg pads, adjust his mask, and plunge into the action. More than anything, he wanted to test his knee to know whether the operation had restored the quick reflexes he needed. Would he still be able to move fast enough during the games and not be paralyzed by pain? Would his body be capable of obeying his brain?

Determined to obtain clear-cut answers to these questions, Jacques was the only player from the regular team to show up at the Canadiens' pre-season training camp in Hull, Quebec. This week was traditionally reserved for evaluating rookies. Without an ounce of

Jacques Plante, the "Masked Marvel."

pride, Jacques wanted to measure himself against the younger players. He was willing to start again from scratch.

Jacques' knee did not let him down. He regained his self-confidence, his smile, and his old zest for giving all he had. Satisfied by this personal tryout, he left to join the Habs' regular training camp, which, exceptionally that year, included an eleven-game tour of Western Canada. Jacques played with so much energy and enthusiasm that he obviously wasn't going to be edged out by either of the two other goaltenders. He demonstrated beyond a doubt that he was still the best, in spite of the gaping hole left by the loss of Doug Harvey, who had gone to play for New York, and to whom some fans had attributed a good part of Jacques Plante's success.

From the very start of the season, the Habs' key players came down with injuries that kept them off the ice. Jean Béliveau, recently promoted team captain, missed 27 games; Dickie Moore, the Canadiens' powerful left-winger, missed 13; and Tom Johnson, the last remaining veteran defenceman for the Habs, missed 8. The team was having trouble getting a cohesive defence line together, and as a result, the burden of keeping the Canadiens in the race that season fell to Jacques. The star who had been sent into mothballs too soon could lift his head proudly. He held his end up skillfully and consistently. In each of the games, he made at least 30 saves although his teammates only managed to take an average of 20 shots at the opponents' net.

It was also during this season that some of the other NHL teams improved their level of play. The

Red Wings had three seasoned forwards in Gordie
Howe, Norm Ullman, and Alex Delvecchio. The Black
Hawks, who had defeated the Canadiens in the playoffs
the previous year, had the unbeatable duo of Bobby
Hull and Stan Mikita. Hull won the scoring championship by establishing his own 50-goal mark. The Habs
stars were embarrassingly absent from offensive play.
But their goalie was once again an impenetrable
fortress, parrying huge numbers of shots. When
Jacques Plante was attacked, he defended himself in
every way he could – both on and off the ice.

Sportswriter Jacques Beauchamp learned this the
hard way. As a reporter for the popular daily, *Montréal
Matin*, he had covered the hockey scene for years. He
travelled everywhere with the Canadiens; he had several friends among the players and was considered part
of the Habs family. At the end of November that year,
writing about a Canadiens-Black Hawks game in
Chicago, he was harshly critical of Jacques' performance. Offended and hurt, Jacques defended himself
in an interview that he granted Robert Desjardins of
Nouvelles Illustrées:

Beauchamp doesn't like me. For example, in
Chicago, when the Hawks tied the score 3-3
with six seconds left in the game, Beauchamp
wrote that I was sleeping for that goal. It
would have been more accurate to say that I
had just done the splits to block a shot with
my skate when I was outplayed by another
torpedo from Bobby Hull, while all of Pilous'
players were piling up in front of me, and my

teammates only had one thought in their minds, which was getting the puck into the Hawks' empty net!

I know that Beauchamp doesn't like me, and it goes back to the best days of Gerry McNeil, his favourite. He is carrying out a campaign against me; he always has something to criticize about my goaltending technique. Frankly, I think we came out of that disastrous trip pretty well, considering the number of players with injuries and our lack of experience in defence. Our boss, Mr. Selke, congratulated us when we got back to Montreal.

Beauchamp hit back in his column:

I admit that McNeil was one of my favourites. I never declared that McNeil was the best goaltender in NHL history, but he was a good guy who never blamed anyone else when the puck got past him, even when it was his teammates' fault. I CAN'T SAY THE SAME OF JACQUES PLANTE....

I have always acknowledged that Plante is a fabulous goaltender. I am not in favour of the mask. I know that Jacques has played a lot of successful games while wearing it, but I still say that he performed more consistently when he didn't wear it during regular games.

As for his goaltending style, I never criticized it. On the contrary, I praised it. I said it many times, and I still say it: hockey needs spectacular athletes like JACQUES PLANTE.

The argument was a symbolic face-off that took up a lot of column space. For a long time, the two men refused to speak to each other. Later, in his book entitled *Sports Are My Life*, Beauchamp confided that a few of the Canadiens players "who complained openly about Jacques Plante's behaviour" had told him: "If you want to help us win the Stanley Cup, roast him in your column."

But in spite of people who criticized or even maligned him, Jacques Plante, 1961 vintage, continued to shine in the nets.

In October, the sports commentators predicted that the Canadiens would finish the season in fourth place, behind Detroit, Chicago, and Toronto. This prediction did not take the masked man's extraordinary comeback into account. It was Jacques Plante alone who carried the team to the finals against formidable odds. He was in full possession of his powers that year and played in all 70 games of the regular season, relegating Cesare Maniago and Charlie Hodge to relative obscurity, as they never had a chance to prove themselves against the Plante phenomenon. His astounding performance allowed the Habs to win their fifth consecutive League championship.

The team was not so fortunate in the finals. After winning the first two games in the playoffs against the Black Hawks, the Habs were bowled over by the brilliant play of Bobby Hull, Stan Mikita, and Glenn Hall in the four subsequent games.

On an individual level, Jacques was elected to the first All-Star team, and won his sixth Vézina Trophy, matching Bill Durnan's record. But he also gained another honour, the most prestigious of them all.

∽

Once the Canadiens had been eliminated, Jacques agreed to participate in a series of lecture-banquets in Western Canada – twenty-one appearances on a tour from Winnipeg to Vancouver. The weather was wonderful that month of May, and the resting goaltender took advantage of the occasion to take a holiday jaunt. He visited the city of Los Angeles and the World's Fair in Seattle. Feeling relaxed, he travelled leisurely from city to city, eventually arriving in Las Vegas.

Jacques had never been a gambler. He always said that it was better to count on one's efforts and talent rather than on luck. Nevertheless, for fun, he sat down at one of the many blackjack tables in the gambling mecca. After half an hour, he had lost about twelve dollars. A new dealer arrived to begin his shift at the table, and stared at Jacques. "It's great to see you here! And you're right to ride on your lucky streak."

Jacques had no idea why the man was talking to him this way; he thought perhaps he'd been mistaken for someone else. "I should try to win my money back, anyway," Jacques answered.

The dealer smiled. "If I were you, I wouldn't worry about that. It's your lucky year." He realized that Jacques didn't catch his meaning and asked, "Well? Aren't you Jacques Plante, the goalie?"

Jacques was astonished: so far from home, in a town where people were much more interested in slot machines, cards, and roulette than in hockey, someone had recognized his face. "You've heard of me?" he asked.

"Of course I have! You had a fantastic season. Really, it *is* your lucky year."

Jacques conceded, "To win the Vézina Trophy, it just takes a lot of work. But to be picked for the first All-Star team, you're right: you have to have a bit of luck for that."

"And the Hart Trophy?" asked the card-dealer. "Was that a combination of both?"

"The Hart Trophy?! *Cercueil de cercueil!*"

Jacques was stunned. Four thousand kilometres from home, a total stranger had just informed him that he had won the trophy that all pro hockey players coveted. Was it true that the panel of NHL sportswriters had finally voted for him? He rushed back to his hotel room to telephone his wife. Jacqueline was relieved to hear his voice, and told him, "It's in all the papers, and the phone hasn't stopped ringing."

He, Jacques Plante, a goaltender, had been awarded the title of most valuable player, over Bobby Hull and his 50 goals, over Doug Harvey and the remarkable job he had done in New York, assuring the Rangers a place in the semi-finals. Jacques couldn't believe it. But he had done even better than they had: he had taken his team to first place, almost singlehandedly.

Jacqueline was literally buried in telegrams that poured in from everywhere to congratulate her husband. Jacques Plante was the fourth goaltender in history to be awarded this great honour, after Roy Worther in 1929, Charlie Rayner in 1950, and Al Rollins in 1954. And since 1962, no other goalie's name has been engraved on the most highly prized trophy of the NHL. Winning the Hart Trophy was the confirmation that Jacques was a truly great hockey player, and, more importantly, that he was by far the most remarkable goaltender of his era. The lad who had dreamed of taking his place between the goalposts for the *bleu-blanc-rouge* had finally attained the zenith of his career, and the recognition of everyone in the sports world.

∞

The following year was not only less spectacular for Jacques, it was very tough on him. He suffered another asthma attack in September. With their goalie out of sorts, the Canadiens had a miserable season. Defenceman Tom Johnson was injured and missed almost half the season. Lou Fontinato's career in the NHL came to an abrupt halt when he received a slamming body check by Lou Hadfield of the Rangers. Jacques missed 14 games and had to be replaced by Cesare Maniago. The Habs finished the season in third place, which, for fans used to cheering on a championship team, was nothing short of a catastrophe.

Throughout that season, relations between Jacques and Toe Blake deteriorated. Blake did not have much sympathy for Jacques' recurring health problems. When Jacques stayed away from practice one

day, the coach was furious. Jacques explained that he
was saving his strength for the games. But even in the
games, Blake was never quite sure whether Jacques
would be able to give his best – especially in Toronto,
where Jacques claimed that he was allergic to the car-
pets at the Royal York Hotel. Now, whenever the Habs
played at Maple Leaf Gardens, Jacques stayed by himself at the Westbury Hotel.

In spite of this arrangement, one evening, Jacques
declared that he could not play the game against the
Leafs that night. Toe Blake was beside himself. "What's
going on, Jacques? You slept at the Westbury last night."

"I know," answered the goaltender, adding, "But I
dreamed that I was at the Royal York!"

The Habs' coach did not appreciate this type of
humour, nor did a few of his teammates, who couldn't
understand why Jacques was getting special treatment.
There were mutterings behind the scenes that he was
eroding team spirit.

The 1962-1963 season was not a good year, neither for Jacques Plante nor for the Canadiens. But in
February, Jacques' name was once again in all the
sports columns. At first, it appeared that he was simply
seeking media attention when he declared that some of
the goals scored in the NHL were illegal. A curious
journalist asked him to develop the subject further.
Jacques explained: "Baseball players have it better than
we do. In any city where they play, home base is always
exactly the same format. In the NHL, the nets aren't all
the same size."

According to Jacques, in Chicago, New York, and
Boston, the goal crossbars were lower than those in the

Detroit, Toronto, and Montreal arenas. The story instantly reached the League managers, who defended themselves in telephone interviews. Lynn Patrick in Boston and Muzz Patrick in New York would have liked nothing better than to laugh the Habs goaltender's statement out of the League, but to be sure of their case, they took measurements first. The result? That troublemaker Jacques Plante was right!

A manufacturing error was discovered: the makers of the Chicago, New York, and Boston nets had soldered the crossbars *between* the two vertical posts instead of on top of them, which meant that those crossbars were a good five centimetres lower than regulation height. The defective products were sent back to the factory, and henceforth, all the nets in the NHL have had exactly the same dimensions.

Reacting to a comment that it hadn't made any difference because both goaltenders in a game had identical nets to defend, Jacques retorted: "*Cercueil!* That's true in a game. But in a season, it makes a big difference. There was a higher mathematical probability that a goalie playing for Chicago, New York, or Boston would win the Vézina trophy. Glenn Hall, for example, played 35 home games in a smaller net, while I played 35 games in a larger net at the Forum."

Once again, Jacques had demonstrated his acute sense of observation and his deep knowledge of hockey. He had first noticed the difference in crossbar heights during a game against the Black Hawks in Chicago. When he took up his position in exactly the same way that he did at the Forum, his back was touching the crossbar. Before going public with his findings, he had carried out the same test at Madison Square Garden and at the Boston Gardens.

This small victory was little more than a diversion, as Jacques' problems remained unresolved. At thirty-four years of age, had the star goalie lost his punch? That was the opinion of some of the commentators, who noted that the Habs had scored the highest number of goals ever that year, and therefore, the team's problems didn't lie with its offence.

The nightmare continued even during the playoffs. Jacques was blamed for the team's rapid elimination in the semifinals against Toronto. With the Canadiens facing sudden death in the fifth game of the series, Jacques was feeling so low that he only went onto the ice for the last few minutes of play. The *bleu-blanc-rouge* suffered a humiliating 5-0 defeat. It was the last straw for Toe Blake: he couldn't keep a man in doubtful health as his number 1 goaltender.

In May, Sam Pollock, Frank Selke's right-hand man, went to talk business with Rangers' manager Muzz Patrick. According to the grapevine, the Canadiens were willing to trade Jacques Plante and Bernie Geoffrion for Lorne "Gump" Worsley, Don McKenney, Dave Balon, and Camille Henry.

Third Period
"Un Canadien Errant…"

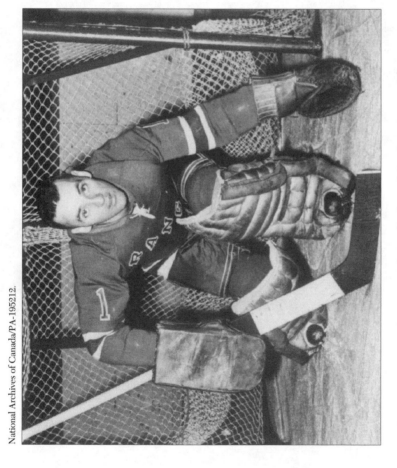

From 1963 to 1965, Jacques Plante tends goal for the New York Rangers.

10

Lonely in Manhattan

Tuesday, June 4, 1963.

When he climbed into his car on a sunny morning in early summer, Jacques Plante had no idea that he was starting out on a very long journey. He had risen early and was looking forward to an enjoyable day. First, he was going to play golf with a teammate, defenceman Jean Gauthier. Then, he was going to the Queen Elizabeth Hotel in downtown Montreal where the managers of all six NHL teams were meeting for the annual draft session. Jacques was feeling no qualms about his future. Playing golf was undoubtedly helping him forget his disastrous season with the Habs.

In the clubhouse locker room, the young Gauthier had other things on his mind besides his still-hesitant golf game. He had just completed his first year with the Canadiens. He loved being with the team, but he knew that its lacklustre performance at the end of the season would result in some changes.

"I'm afraid I'm going to be traded," he confided to the goaltender. "You're going to the meeting today. Maybe if you said a word to the management..."

Jacques promised to do what he could.

Just after twelve noon, he got into his car and drove in the direction of downtown Montreal. He was listening to a Dalida song that he liked when a news flash interrupted the program.

"Ladies and gentlemen, we are interrupting our regular broadcast to bring you a special news bulletin: the Montreal Canadiens hockey club have just signed the most spectacular agreement in the history of the NHL. They have traded seven players, including their star goaltender, Jacques Plante, to the New York Rangers."

Jacques slammed on the brakes and pulled the car over to the side of the road. His heart was beating hard and he wondered if he was dreaming. But he knew that he was awake: everything around him was sharp and clear. He turned up the volume with a shaking hand.

"The man that many experts have called the greatest goaltender in modern hockey is going to the Rangers, along with centre Phil Goyette and defenceman Don Marshall. In exchange, the Canadiens are getting goaltender Lorne 'Gump' Worsley and forwards Dave Balon, Léon Rochefort, and Len Ronson, all players from the minor league."

Jacques was in shock. He hesitated, trying to decide what to do. Should he give in to his feelings and go home? But where would that get him? He would just have to sit there, biting his nails until the official phone call came. No, that wasn't his style. He braced himself.

Since he had first donned skates, since he had first watched a puck hurtling towards him, he had never imagined himself in anything other than a Canadiens uniform. In that sense, the news was a personal catastrophe, the end of a dream that had been the underlying motivation of his whole life. On the other hand, Jacques had never let himself be defeated; he had always viewed adversity as a challenge and had gone to meet it with his eyes wide open. It is the main characteristic of a good goaltender: the determination to hold the fort at all costs, in any situation. It is also the essence of valour.

Jacques started up his car and continued driving in the same direction. He would show up at the Queen Elizabeth as planned.

The radical trade in the works had, as might be expected, given birth to a slew of rumours, but no one had imagined that so many heads would fall. Doug Harvey last year, and now Jacques Plante; who would be next? What would remain of the great club now that it had cut all the core players loose? Bold headlines expressed outrage and doubt:

A stroke of genius, or insanity? The experts are pessimistic.

Have the Canadiens paid too high a price in reorganizing the team?

The club's decision was either defended or panned:

Jacques Plante had a lot of trouble standing up to pressure. – Toe Blake

Jacques Plante is the greatest goalkeeper I have ever seen in action. – Chuck Rayner, former goaltender and member of the New York Rangers organization.

The Rangers have struck it rich: Selke has given them the winner of six VÉZINA TRO-PHIES. – Phil Séguin, *La Patrie*.

If the Canadiens got the best of the bargain, it will only show in a few years. – André Trudelle, *La Presse*

Still in doubt about Jacques' departure from the team, the same *La Presse* writer commented:

Just one month ago, general manager Frank Selke said to us in his office: 'Jacques Plante in good health is our man. We're not inter-ested in a sick Jacques Plante.'

We have the impression that general manager Frank Selke, and many fans as well, have never understood the 'Plante case.'

He was criticized for being a showman (Plante himself admitted the truth of this), for saying that he wasn't well before every

important game, for blaming the defencemen
for most of the goals that he let in.

Between ourselves, those were harmless
foibles that we should have accepted as a
tradeoff for keeping a great champion, who,
like Doug Harvey, belongs to the Rangers now.

In *Montréal-Matin*, popular sportswriter Jerry
Trudel offered an insightful analysis:

> · PLANTE ALWAYS ACTED
> IN THE TEAM'S BEST INTEREST
> It is my humble opinion that the Canadiens'
> managers have cut off their noses to spite
> their faces by trading Jacques Plante, the
> greatest goaltender in NHL history, as well as
> one of the most intelligent observers and stu-
> dents of the game of hockey....
>
> It may be that Plante, in the eyes of cer-
> tain people, is guilty of having a strong mind
> and character. It appears that, since he began
> with the Canadiens, there has been a deliber-
> ate effort to suppress his individuality and fit
> him into a rigid mould. It was Dick Irvin who
> made him stop wearing his tuque during
> games, a harmless bit of colour that added to
> the team's personality....
>
> When Irvin was coach, Plante accepted
> everything without saying a word. But as the
> years passed, and he proved himself as an
> extraordinary goaltender, Jacques refused to
> meekly accept everything he was told,

especially when he was convinced that it wasn't in his best interest.

One day, Plante decided to wear a face-mask. There was an immediate uproar and some of his employers teased him about it. Others even ridiculed him. But it didn't get them anywhere. Jacques stuck to his guns, even when people tried to convince him that every one of his mistakes was caused by wearing the mask....

He embarrassed the NHL authorities last year by proving that the nets were not all standard size in the League. In other words, when something was wrong, Plante, as a person of conscience, refused to say that everything was all right.

The same applied to his physical condition. Whenever Jacques Plante felt ill, he said it out loud, and when he felt that he couldn't carry out his job to the best of his ability, he didn't hesitate to ask to be replaced....

But it seems that his independent spirit and outspokenness did not please everyone, and a lot of people began to find him quite troublesome and willful. This was because they refused to believe in the sincerity of the man, although he had shown his immense integrity a long time ago.

I don't know the reasons behind trading Plante for Worsley, but I tend to think that Jacques was a thorn in the side of many people who are used to getting their own way all the time.

While the commentators and fans wrung their hands or scratched their heads over this surprise move, thoughtful analyst and talented writer Louis Chantigny dug a little deeper to try to get to the bottom of it. He was given a disturbing answer by Frank Selke himself: "We had to make a definite stand and give an example that would create a stir. Some of our players were getting too rich, too indulged by honours and glory. When we told them that they might be traded if their playing was not up to par, they refused to take us seriously and figured that they were assured of finishing their careers with the Canadiens. Maybe now, they'll understand that the same thing could happen to any of them. Next season, I expect that Marshall and Goyette will play better for the Rangers than Rochefort, Balon, and Ronson will play for us. I don't have any illusions about that, but I had to rebuild the team with an eye to the future."

Selke confessed to Chantigny: "If Plante plays his best for the Rangers, and Worsley plays his best for us, we will still be getting the worst of the bargain."

The reporter felt outraged. Selke remained silent for a moment. Then, in three blunt sentences, he revealed his true thoughts on the matter.

"Jacques Plante is an extrovert who can't put his personal interest aside for the benefit of the team. In the circumstances, no matter how brilliant a goaltender he may be, it was better that he left. That's what you can say in the papers."

Chantigny continued his investigation and went to interview Jacques at home, to hear his version of events. Of course, the fact that Jacques was responsible for the team's pension fund and that he and Don Marshall were the Canadiens' representatives in the Players' Association had affected his relationship with the club management. But the problem went deeper than that.

Jacques opened his heart to the journalist. "Last year, I was reprimanded several times, and I'm not surprised that I was traded. Selke blamed me for everything, *cercueil!* He criticized me for talking too much, for going out of my crease too often, for lifting my arms up in the air when we won – if it wasn't one thing, it was another. According to him, I crouched down too low in front of the net; I wasn't covering the corners well enough. Or he said I was causing too many stops in play when we were short-handed, when in fact, my teammates had asked me to do it so that they could get their wind back. Frank Selke would call me into his office for any little thing. I had gone in there so many times in the last few years that I felt like I worked there! Underneath it all was the fact that Selke wanted to turn me into somebody else."

It was true that a deep misunderstanding had grown up between the two men. It was, more accurately, a generational conflict between two refined hockey analysts – one who defended the traditional way of playing, and one who had always been a great innovator. Louis Chantigny expressed it this way:

Like all innovators who revolutionize an
established pattern to create a new one
adapted to their colossal scale, Plante has
always been the target of sarcasm and criticism.... A thousand and one examples show
that it is not always easy, and that it can be
aggravating to be around creative minds.
Jacques Plante and Frank Selke were like fire
and water, and countless incidents showed it!
But what did this personality conflict matter
as long as Jacques Plante was performing the
difficult task that was assigned to him with
such brio? And how is it that a good psychol-
ogist like Frank Selke didn't understand that
a dull conformist could never have become
an incomparable goaltender and the greatest
innovator in the entire history of hockey?

For Jacques' family, the news of the trade had the
effect of an earthquake. Comfortably installed in the
suburbs of Montreal, the Plantes had no desire to leave
their home. Jacqueline decided that it was best for her
to stay in Canada with the couple's two sons while
Jacques was in New York tending net for the Rangers.

From then onward, Jacques' lot would be that of
those visionaries who have strived for change, whose
one aim is to go further, in spite of opposition from all
sides, even if the consequence is exile and loneliness.

That summer, Jacques was as active as usual. As
he truly enjoyed amateur sports, he umpired at Pee-
Wee baseball tournaments and played golf regularly.
He received a much bigger volume of mail than at any

other period in his career. On his typewriter, he answered every one of the fans who had written, concerned about his future. It seemed that he had never been so loved as now, when he was leaving the country.

Characteristically, in New York, the comments on Jacques' approaching debut with the Rangers were uniformly positive. Newspapermen in the Big Apple love winners, whether they are artists or tycoons: they make good copy. And when these heroes are from the sports world, the enthusiasm doubles. Although hockey wasn't usually given much space in the papers, especially in the middle of the baseball season, Jacques Plante's arrival was featured on the front of the sports section. The Rangers' management left no stone unturned as far as publicity was concerned: a red carpet was rolled down for the man that New Yorkers now considered the uncontested top goaltender in pro hockey.

Jacques was not indifferent to this show of adulation, nor to the fact that when he signed his name to a contract guaranteeing him a salary of $24,000 a year, he had become the highest-paid goaltender in history. He was also pleased that would be reunited with his old buddy, Doug Harvey, with whom he had shared so many exciting victories.

And Jacques talked. Still hurting from the trade, he spoke frankly about his aims and ambitions for the season. The challenge was daunting: the Rangers, who had been shuffling along in the NHL for years, faced a steep climb to get to the top. The team would reach the playoffs, Jacques promised, adding that the same might not apply to the Canadiens that year.

He even dared to make a public evaluation of the top scorers on his former team. According to Jacques, the Habs only had three sure bets since Dickie Moore had announced his departure, but even those three had problems. Jean Béliveau was ill and had slowed down, Bernie Geoffrion didn't hit the puck as hard as before, and Henri "The Pocket Rocket" Richard missed many scoring opportunities by trying to make the opponents' goalie come out of his net too often.

Naturally, due note was taken of Jacques' comments in Montreal.

∞

Jacques' new season began in Chicago on October 9, 1963. He was injured in the second period of the game and was unable to stop the Rangers from losing 3-1.

His appearance at the Forum scheduled for the following Saturday was the news event of the week in Montreal. Jacques' declarations seemed to have roused his former teammates. It was an emotion-filled encounter, and some commentators even saw it as a vendetta. When the two teams met, several individuals had their own personal accounts to settle. The raging Canadiens stormed their ex-goaltender's net from the first seconds of the game. Jacques faced a veritable bombardment: 59 shots in one game! Anyone but Jacques Plante would have let in at least a dozen shots. However, not even a champion is infallible.

In the end, the Habs won 6-2. The scorers: Geoffrion with 2 goals, and Jean Béliveau, Robert Rousseau, Dave Balon, and John Ferguson with one apiece. The Habs were glad to prove to their fans, to themselves, and especially to Jacques Plante that they were still a power to be reckoned with. But in a paradoxical tribute, Jacques was cheered by the same Montreal crowd that had booed him in the Canadiens net a few months before. Wearing the white Rangers' sweater that night, he had captured the hearts of the often-fickle public. The sports world is truly bizarre at times.

After playing two games, Jacques realized that he had faced 99 shots! It was going to be a long, tough season. In spite of this formidable beginning, he managed to obtain a shutout in the first game played at home in Madison Square Garden, a 3-0 victory over Detroit. Named as first star of the game, he skated onto centre ice holding his mask at the end of his outstretched arm amid a huge ovation. Having blocked 33 shots with acrobatic prowess, he waved to the crowd as if he were a Broadway star...and that's precisely what he was during his time with the Rangers.

∞

The campaign would not be easily fought: the conqueror was still fragile. During a game in Toronto at the end of October, Jacques suffered another asthma attack and had to go home to Montreal to recuperate.

Although he was adored by the New York public for his showmanship and appreciated by the press for always providing good quotes, Jacques was not really happy playing for the Rangers. He missed his family. It was the first time that he had lived away from them and the solitary life was difficult to bear. After the euphoria of the first few weeks of the season, he discovered that he fitted the description of the typical lonely stranger in Manhattan.

There was another problem that was even more difficult to ignore: Jacques the perfectionist often found himself grinding his teeth at the way the coach managed the Rangers. Although he had not always agreed with Toe Blake and Frank Selke, Jacques was aware that both of them had an innate sense of the game of hockey and knew how to manage championship teams. In the Big Apple, Red Sullivan was miles away from being a good strategist. In fact, his coaching career was no more brilliant than his career as a player; he had been a steady but uninspired centre-wing, and his achievements as an NHL coach never rose above mediocre. It was not surprising that Jacques, with his exceptional talent as a game analyst who noticed every detail of play, saw things from a different point of view than his coach.

One night at about eleven o'clock, Sullivan made the mistake of telephoning his goaltender to verify if he was observing the team curfew rule. The veteran NHL player could hardly believe his ears. He answered Sullivan curtly: "*Cercueil!* I've been in bed since nine o'clock, and I just managed to get to sleep. Now I won't be able to fall asleep again for another three or four hours. I don't want you to call me again. Ever."

And George "Red" Sullivan never did.

Another thing that perturbed Jacques' routine-loving nature was the fact that the team was obliged to practise in distant arenas whenever the ice in Madison

Square Garden was preempted by a show. Thus, when the team was at home, Jacques often had to travel out to Long Island to the practices. This meant that the morning after an exhausting game, he would have to leave home at 8:30 a.m. and only return at 5:30 in the evening. As a result, he felt tired all the time and did not have a chance to get his strength back for the games. His performance in the nets suffered accordingly.

Jacques had the impression that he was far away from everything that he cared about. Although a few French Canadians played for the Rangers, he did not associate closely with any of them. Most of the time, he declined to attend the dinners and parties that were organized for the players and their wives. He experienced the painful loneliness of an outsider, a loneliness that was interrupted by rare sparks of glory. On March 7th and 8th, he played exceptional games against the Canadiens – two vintage Jacques Plante performances. The first game was a 3-2 victory at the Forum on a Saturday night, and the second was a no-goal tie at Madison Square Garden.

Unfortunately, the Rangers (without Doug Harvey, who had only played 14 games before being sent down to the Quebec City Aces), finished the regular season in fifth place, and therefore did not qualify for the playoffs. The season's overall results were considered negative, as 242 goals had been scored against the team – a higher number than any other team in the League. Jacques' personal results: 3 shutouts, 220 goals allowed in 65 games, and a 3.38 goals-against average, a lamentable career high. The Canadiens, on the other hand, finished in first place. However, the great team had had to be shaken up to get there.

∞

In spite of some bad moments in the NHL, Jacques never stopped enjoying sports during his summer vacations in Quebec. He still felt the need to be active, and to be totally involved in a game – to feed on the electricity generated by competition.

The summer following Jacques Plante's first season with the Rangers, a group of sportsmen decided to revive the traditional Native-American game that had drawn enthusiastic crowds until the 1930s: lacrosse. The game resembles hockey in many ways. The principle is straightforward: the players must catch and hold a leather ball in a net attached to the end of a metre-long stick (the crosse) and hurl it into the opposing team's goal. A lacrosse field is the same size as a hockey rink. There are six players: five forwards and the goalkeeper. The players are not as well protected as hockey players: they wear light helmets and running shoes.

There were four teams in the revived organization: the Montreal Nationals, the Caughnawaga Indians, the Ville St. Pierre team, and the Drummondville Athletics. The league needed a star attraction to get off the ground. One of the promoters, who included sportswriters Michel and Gilles Blanchard, had the idea of inviting Jacques Plante to join the Nationals. After all, in his younger days, Jacques had been a champion lacrosse player both in Shawinigan and Quebec City. But how could they lure a pro like Jacques, who watched his money closely and who was under contract to the New York Rangers? The most courageous of the organizers went ahead and telephoned him. Jacques was enchanted by the proposal. He immediately replied that he would ask Muzz Patrick for the necessary permission. It was granted.

Jacques was willing to do anything for the sake of sports. He agreed to play for the minimum salary, ten dollars a game, and to bring his own soap and towel to the games. He was ready and willing to give all he had in his new role. Of course, goalkeeping in lacrosse is completely different from minding a hockey net. Even if Jacques still wore a mask, he couldn't come out of his net. Also, the lacrosse goalie can't stop the play, but has to relaunch the attack as soon as he catches a shot.

Soon, Jacques was back in the Montreal Forum, tending goal for the Nationals and wearing a sweater that bore an uncanny resemblance to his red, white, and blue uniform of yore. More than just a figurehead, Jacques performed spectacularly for his team.

Gilles Blanchard was impressed by Jacques' generosity and lack of condescension during his stint with the Nationals. After Jacques' death, he wrote:

> Plante, the big star, had become a member of the Nationals, and was the best advertisement that the team and the sport could have wished for.
>
> He gave his best in the practices we held in the yard of the Collège Ste. Marie, in the long trips in school buses, and in the endless interviews that he granted.

Plante brought along his soap and towel like the rest of the team members, was paid his ten dollars a game like all the others, and showed the same schoolboy enthusiasm....

And what a professional! He had the statistical low-down on every player, knew their feints, their every strength and weakness. Once the question of salary was out of the way, he dedicated himself, body and soul, to the team, just like in his greatest Stanley Cup years.

I remember very well that when the coach was ready to end to the practice, Jacques would prolong an already exhausting session, saying, "One more ball into the goal and then to the showers."

Then Jacques would block throws over and over again. He knew our playing abilities better than we did ourselves. We would never go back to the dressing-room without his O.K.

The summer after that, Jacques played four games for the Caughnawaga Indians. Unfortunately, the league was soon dissolved, but it certainly wasn't for any lack of dedication on Jacques Plante's part.

The Rangers did not achieve any better results in the 1964-1965 season. Jacques was having new problems.

Living away from home, he felt as if he were struggling through a thick fog, step by uncertain step.

The sports world is disloyal to its prodigal sons, even those who have revolutionized the sport and given it everything they had, all their hopes, talent, and brilliance.

At the beginning of the season, Jacques was sent down to the Baltimore Clippers until he had recuperated from an injury to his right knee. Baltimore hockey fans were given full value. Like all those who had come to appreciate Jacques Plante's greatness, they were treated to spectacular saves. Jacques went back and forth between the Rangers and the Clippers. He played only 33 games in the Rangers' net that season, and for the second year in a row, his goals-against average was above 3 per game.

In June 1965, less than forty-eight hours before the annual NHL draft session, Emile "The Cat" Francis, the Rangers' new manager, called reporters to a press conference where it was announced that goaltender Jacques Plante was hanging up his mask and skates and would not be playing for the Rangers next season.

Jacques had had an operation on his right knee; it was not yet clear if it had been successful and if he would be in shape for the season. Once again, Jacques was obliged to start from scratch. However, the predominating reason that he had decided to leave the sport he loved had to do with his family. Jacqueline had become depressed during her husband's absence and had lost a lot of weight. Jacques realized that he should return home to be with her and their two sons. Michel, fourteen, and Richard, ten, were at an age when they particularly needed their father. Also, although he never voiced the thought, Jacques felt that he had lost some of his spark by playing with diminished physical capacities for a second-rate team.

The Quebec City Aces of the American Hockey League saw a golden opportunity and immediately offered Jacques a yearly salary of $25,000 to play for them – with the incentive that he was exempted from practices. However, Jacques turned this friendly offer down. Molson Breweries, owners of the Canadiens, had offered him a job as promotion manager; Jacques decided to accept it. He could live at home while still being able to support his family.

In any case, Jacques was far from poverty-stricken. He owned the family home in Laval-des-Rapides, outside Montreal, as well as three revenue properties of four apartments each. Jacques was also looking forward to enjoying one of his favourite hobbies: oil painting.

All sorts of rumours about Jacques were flying around the hockey world. Punch Imlach, the Toronto Maple Leafs coach, a man who had always known how to get the best out of his veteran players, declared that he would hire Jacques if the Rangers, who were obviously in trouble as far as net-minding was concerned, would release him from his contract. Jacques was well aware that several NHL teams were interested in him. It was gratifying, of course, but his New York experience was still too fresh in his mind. He needed time for his wounds to heal. It was vital for him to return to ordinary life.

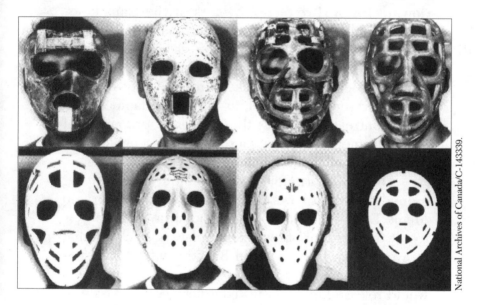

The different masks designed and used by Jacques Plante during his career.

11

The Red Night

A new Molson Brewery representative was touring the province of Quebec: his name was Jacques Plante. At last – perhaps for the first time in his life – Jacques relaxed, taking life as it came. Looking back, it seemed as if he had never done this before. From his earliest childhood, he remembered having to overcome one obstacle after another to escape from poverty and to win a place in the world. Like all true champions, Jacques was proud: he had aimed for the top and had reached it. Yet he had always known that it wouldn't last forever. Even with the most determined efforts to prolong this euphoric plateau, time catches up with everyone; it is impossible, even for the best, to stay at the zenith for more than a brief moment. What goes up must come down – no matter how high the mountain peak that you have scaled and claimed, no matter how great the dream that has inspired you and your fellow human beings.

Wherever he went, the Molson's rep had his hand shaken and was asked for his autograph. He had an easy manner and a natural charm that held him in good stead in his new job. He enjoyed being recognized and loved to talk to people. When Jacques Plante told a story, it was never short. He was used to being a public figure by now. He wasn't intimidated by being the centre of attention in a crowd or by meeting new people – and in these months, he met a lot of them. Along with Maurice Richard, Jacques Plante remained the best-known hockey player of his time. Each in his own special way, both the Rocket and Jacques contributed to making their sport better known. More than simply by their skill, they had elevated hockey's standards of excellence: Richard by his wholeheartedness and his fiery playing style, and Jacques Plante by his intelligence and imagination.

In a few brief years, hockey had suddenly grown beyond its original boundaries. NHL managers were already negotiating the first major league expansion. At the start of the 1967-1968 season, there were new teams all over the continent, as far as Los Angeles and Oakland on the Pacific Coast. This was partly due to the achievements of Maurice Richard and Jacques Plante.

Now that he represented the company that owned the Montreal Canadiens, Jacques was associated with the Habs' days of glory wherever he went. He played in several promotional golf tournaments and still excelled at that game; he also played tennis, improving steadily. He was free to live in the modest way that he had chosen.

However, deep within himself, Jacques was torn apart. He knew that he should appreciate his graceful retirement from professional sports, but he wasn't satisfied watching other people play. He had started so young that being active in sports had always been the centre of his existence. Now, when he watched a hockey game, he would get butterflies in his stomach and twitches in his legs. When the season recommenced that year, his way of combatting his restlessness was to play in the Quebec Old Timers League. Jacques' passion for hockey was alive and well, and he still adored stopping pucks.

It was exceedingly difficult to get rid of a deeply ingrained habit, and everyone could see that what the Molson Brewery rep missed most was playing top-level hockey. The Junior Canadiens coach, Scotty Bowman, already a wily strategist and proud competitor, knew it better than anyone else.

The Soviet National Team was about to arrive for its second North American tour. It hadn't yet become the team that would teach a lesson to the NHL pros in the 1970s, but it was nonetheless a very smooth, well-trained club with fast, skillful players in excellent physical condition, each one with a precise role that he carried out effectively. The Russians were dangerous. They had won several world amateur championships as well as the gold medal at the 1964 Winter Olympics.

And, like the year before, the Soviets were going to play against the Junior Canadiens. In 1964, the

Juniors had been helped by several NHL veterans who were now with the Quebec City Aces: Gump Worsley, Doug Harvey, Red Berenson, Léon Rochefort, John Hanna, and Bill Sutherland. The Russians had beaten the Juniors 6-5 in 1964. Scotty Bowman did not want a repeat red victory on December 15, 1965.

This time, the Junior Canadiens included some very young players who would later make their mark in the National League: defencemen Serge Savard and Carol Vadnais, forwards Larry Pleau and Christian Bordeleau, and last but not least, centre Jacques Lemaire. The Russian managers agreed to allow the Juniors to add five players from the Central League Houston Apollos to their ranks; thus, the lineup would include Noël Picard, Jean Gauthier, Bill Inglis, Norman Dennis, and André Boudrias. The only missing ingredient was a high-calibre goaltender.

Scotty Bowman thought of Jacques Plante. Newly retired, he might agree to play. Bowman talked it over with team president David Molson and general manager Sam Pollock. Neither of them saw any reason why Jacques shouldn't play.

They called Jacques just one week before the first game against the Soviet team was to take place. How could a hockey-crazy athlete like Jacques have turned away from this exciting challenge? After ironing out a few formalities with the Rangers, who still owned him, and having received permission from Molson Breweries, Jacques began practising. He needed to sharpen his reflexes and regain his suppleness. He had lost some of his edge in his games with the Old Timers, in which slapshots and bodychecks were prohibited.

But what was the legendary Jacques Plante doing in this situation? He had voluntarily retired. He had nothing left to prove as far as hockey was concerned. By playing in this type of highly publicized confrontation, he had little to gain but a lot to lose.

People's curiosity got the better of them when it was announced that Jacques was going to play; it was an unexpected chance to see the famous goaltender wearing the Habs' uniform for a last time. The promotional machine was effective: 10,000 fans had been expected, but 14,981 people showed up to fill the hockey temple on St. Catherine Street.

The Soviets arrived at the Forum with three victories on Canadian soil under their belts. They had just trounced the Canadian National Team 4-0 in London, Ontario, after having beaten them 8-6 in Quebec City on the preceding Sunday.

In Montreal, the first period was played at a very fast pace. The "little" Canadiens were clearly finding it difficult to ward off the Russians' methodical attack. The red-uniformed players succeeded in making several electrifying breakaways, but were blocked by a vigilant Jacques Plante who brought the fans to their feet by a succession of acrobatic saves. He seemed to always be in the right place to stop the opponents' accurate shots on the short, fast passes from their teammates. For a goaltender who hadn't played a "real" game in over eight months, Jacques demonstrated astonishingly good timing. At the end of the period, both teams left the ice without having scored, but Jacques had stopped 13 shots, 5 more than his Russian counterpart, Viktor Zinger.

In the second period, the Junior Habs' defence was more alert. The game became a more balanced struggle, with the Juniors covering their adversaries closely. But in the middle of the period, during a penalty to Noël Picard, defenceman Vladimir Brezhnev took a screened shot from the blue-line. Jacques didn't see it in time, and the Russians scored their first goal.

In North American hockey, a one-goal lead never seems insurmountable, but the Soviets were so quick and so much in control of the puck that this single goal gave them palpable confidence. Jacques exhorted his teammates from the net to keep up the fight.

In the third period, Scotty Bowman's team redoubled its efforts. André Boudrias and Serge Savard forced the Russian goaltender to make some difficult saves, but it was Larry Pleau who finally scored at 7 minutes and 42 seconds into the period, on a pass by Norm Ferguson. The relieved Juniors might have been content to accept a tied end count, but they realized that to simply stay on the defensive against such a well-oiled machine was altogether too risky. Finally, with 30 seconds left in the game, the Junior Habs got an opening: Bill Inglis received a pass from André Boudrias and took a shot. It was blocked by Zinger, but right-winger Bill Dennis flipped the deflected puck past the goalie. The crowd went crazy. Victory for the home team was imminent, but the Junior Habs still had to hold out for another half-minute. The Russians took their goaltender off the ice. With less than ten seconds left in the game, Vaniamin Alexandrov broke away: Jacques, as quick as he had ever been in his heyday, made a superb save. The final score: Junior Canadiens 2, Soviets 1.

As soon as the siren sounded, Jacques was mobbed by his teammates. Serge Savard and Noël Picard lifted him onto their shoulders and the Montreal Forum shook with one of the loudest ovations in its history. Carried in triumph, Jacques waved to the fans, mask in hand. He had carried off an almost perfect performance – a signature Jacques Plante performance.

At the entrance of the Forum, everyone was talking about him. The spectators of this thrilling match were all agreed that Jacques Plante could hold his own on any NHL team. He was still the best and the most spectacular hockey goaltender in the world. The Russians' No. 11, Alexander Almetov, had a good reason to say it: all four of his shots, three of which were taken when he was alone in front of the net, had been stopped by Jacques.

In the dressing room, even with all the bright young hopes surrounding him, Jacques did not feel like a patriarch. He was simply an athlete who, once again, had given everything he had for the love of the sport.

"For me, this is one of the happiest moments since I began playing hockey," declared the sweat-drenched goaltender. "I wasn't playing for Jacques Plante; I was playing for Canada."

Even if this was the first defeat in their Canadian tour, the Russian players were thrilled to have played against a true hockey legend. Their coach, Anatoly Tarasov, was effusive in his praise.

"You want me to talk about Jacques Plante? We only knew him by name. Tonight, not only did we meet him, we felt his presence. I'd like to ask you to thank him – to say thank you to Jacques Plante on behalf of all of us. I am speechless when I see him play. I hope I can say that the Russian team deserved to meet such a goaltender. It was a great honour for us to play against him."

Later on, analysing the game more calmly, Jacques explained how he had figured out the opponents' individual strategies even though he had never seen any of them play before. He had watched their feet: the position of their skates was his gauge, the tangible reference he had chosen to focus on. By doing this, he could predict the trajectory of each of the shots that were coming at him and would move into position to cover the angle correctly. In that one isolated game on that December evening, his prodigious knowledge of hockey had allowed him to decode an unfamiliar adversary's game. In sixty minutes, he had brilliantly demonstrated the fruit of years of accumulated observation and experience.

∞

The day after the game, Jacques went back to work for the Molson company, as usual. He presided over amateur tournaments and advised young players at several hockey schools. Beside giving them the benefit of his vast experience, he tried to inspire them to play for the love of the game instead of just playing to win. To Jacques, sport was a noble pursuit that merited being practised for its own sake – and Jacques knew what the love of the game was all about.

12

The Amazing Comeback

June 6, 1967.

With the annual NHL draft session scheduled to take place, the most ambitious expansion plan in sports history became a reality. The desire to reach new markets began a process that indelibly transformed hockey. The Golden Age of the six NHL teams now belonged to the past. NHL owners and managers paid court to the West Coast, the land of Hollywood super-productions, and the mythical destination of gold diggers and adventurers.

The "Go west, young man!" of the previous century had become a rallying cry for a new kind of pioneer, one who carried a pair of hockey skates laced

National Archives of Canada/PA-185907.

Drafted by the St. Louis Blues, Jacques Plante makes a comeback
in 1968 and wins his seventh Vézina Trophy.

together and slung over a hockey stick instead of the proverbial bundle of clothes tied to the end of a pole. The six original NHL teams now formed the Eastern Conference of the League; six new teams were created to make up the Western Conference. The western newcomers were the Philadelphia Flyers, the Los Angeles Kings, the St. Louis Blues, the Minnesota North Stars, the Pittsburgh Penguins, and the Oakland Seals – and there were plans to add still more teams to the League. Before this, 108 people had been on the NHL payroll; now there were 216, not counting the managers, coaches, scouts, and the rest of the army that worked behind the scenes. Although more people were interested in hockey than ever before and players could move easily from coast to coast, the core of the talent became diluted. Star players did not suddenly appear to fill the new slots. On the positive side, it meant that more young players could aspire to reach the big league in a shorter time. Also, veteran players, who had learned the ropes of the game while freezing their toes and ears on outdoor rinks, could now hope to prolong their careers by a few extra years, while taking advantage of the slightly higher salaries that came with the whole expansion project.

The new contracts only protected a select few players on each team, and thus, many of the old soldiers of the NHL became available for trades. The luckier ones went to warm themselves in southern climes. Dave Balon expatriated himself to Minnesota; the venerable Andy Bathgate went to Pittsburgh, and defencemen Bobby Baun and Kent Douglas signed with Oakland. Certain clubs gave a higher priority to establishing a solid base by obtaining a good goal-keeper. The Philadelphia Flyers chose two promising youngsters, Bernie Parent and Doug Favell. However, experienced NHL goalies were the targets of choice. The ever-solid Glenn Hall opted to play for St. Louis, leaving work on the farm for a later date.

Jacques, always an attentive observer of the hockey scene, noted that one of the idols of his youth, Terry Sawchuk – whose brilliant playing for the Maple Leafs had prevented the Stanley Cup from gracing the World's Fair in Montreal that year – was first draft choice by the Los Angeles Kings. Sawchuk was actually the same age as Jacques, as was Gump Worsley, who remained with the Canadiens. So many radical changes in the organization of the sport made Jacques rethink his own plans. Two years in retirement had taken him away from hockey too long for him to be considered first pick by the managers of the new teams. Jacques was happy to be a Molson's ambassador and was enjoying his present life. But his heart still belonged to hockey.

∽

At the beginning of that 1967-1968 season, Jacques received a phone call: it was a hockey proposition. He was all ears; how could a lifelong hockey lover have resisted the temptation? Once again, there were comments and speculation in the sports pages when Jacques asked his employer for time off to join the Oakland Seals' training camp in Port Huron, Michigan.

After a few days, he was the centre of attention and the big question mark at the camp. Rumours abounded that Jacques Plante was going to make a comeback with the California team. He denied it energetically. "No, *cercueil!* I just came to help out my ex-teammate, Bert Olmstead. He asked me to train his goaltenders. There definitely won't be a comeback."

The coaching help that Jacques had referred to took on an unconventional allure as the training camp evolved: he seemed to be teaching mainly by example. No one was surprised to see him in the Seals' nets in an out-of-season game against the Los Angeles Kings. He let in a couple of shots by Lowell McDonald and Eddie Joyal before giving up his place to rookie goalie Gary Smith at mid-game.

"Wouldn't you call that a comeback?" a reporter queried.

"I just wanted to see if I was still capable of stopping pucks in the NHL," Jacques answered. "Now I know I can."

Was there a basis of truth in the rumours, then? As is often the case, the sportswriters had jumped the gun. Jacques finished his three-week stint with the Seals and returned to Montreal, satisfied by the experience. When the reporters pestered him, he declared that it would take ten years for one of the newly created expansion teams to win the Stanley Cup. His reasoning was simple: each of the fledgling teams depended on one top scorer, whereas the long-established teams like the Canadiens and the Black Hawks each possessed up to eight sure goal-getters.

"The only way the new teams can keep from being overwhelmed is by developing good defensive strategies, but that's not the way to win cups."

Jacques' analysis proved astonishingly accurate. During the ensuing seasons, the expansion teams that did practise a defensive game were the most successful ones. He had also predicted a 60-goal season for Bobby Hull, and the formidable No. 9 of the Hawks scored 58 times in the 1968-1969 season.

Jacques went back to work at Molson. For once, Lady Rumour had missed the mark, but she would have a chance to redeem herself.

∞

Jacques kept abreast of developments in hockey through his job. At the same time, some of the League managers remained aware that he could still perform in the nets. The fact that he was not yet out of the running in big league hockey came to light when Emile Francis, the Rangers' general manager and coach, called on Jacques to solve a problem during the 1967-1968 season; Jacques was still under contract to the New York team. The coach had noticed that his regular goalie, Ed Giacomin, did not perform as well when the team faced the Chicago Black Hawks. The usually dependable Giacomin seemed to falter particularly when playing in the Windy City Stadium. One day, Francis called Jacques in Montreal.

"Jacques, can you do me a favour?"

"What is it?"

"We still have five games left to play against Chicago. I'd like you to tend goal for us in those games. I'm sure you could be in shape if you trained in Buffalo for a week."

Buffalo, Chicago – the very names of those cities evoked cherished memories for Jacques. In Buffalo, he had won the hearts of the American fans, and in Chicago, he had played his first NHL playoffs. However, he still hesitated. The contract itself was attractive, and five games did not mean a whole season, but he balked at the prospect of leaving his family and his job at Molson. Besides, even if the Rangers had definitely improved since his days in the Big Apple, he did not look back on that period with any great fondness. He had been so lonely in New York. He did not want to go through that again, even for the pleasure of measuring himself a few more times against Stan Mikita, Ken Wharram, and Dennis and Bobby Hull, who were wreaking havoc in the League.

Inevitably, with this kind of solicitation being pressed on him, the idea of a comeback gradually took shape in his mind. During a visit to Ottawa, he ran into an NHL scout who asked him, banteringly, if he didn't want to return to the NHL on a more regular basis.

Jacques replied in the same joking manner. But when he went home, he mentioned the exchange to Jacqueline. She knew very well that her husband was longing to get back into pro hockey.

"I'm better now," she told him. "And you're in good condition. If you feel like trying your luck…"

His luck! Luck hardly entered into Jacques' analytical playing style. For every shot against him, he prepared a strategy based on his formidable memory of each player's style, on his sense of the game, and on his characteristic combativeness. Every time, he calculated with lightning speed exactly how he would block a shot, how he would stretch out his leg, when he would skate beyond the goal crease to pass the puck to a defence-man, and which instructions he would shout to a team-mate. He anticipated every breakaway, every pass. He knew all the tactics by heart.

To return to the rink, Jacques' body had to be up to par. It hardly seemed worth the effort of getting back into condition to play only five games. But if, on the other hand, he could play a more reasonable num-ber of games, dividing the task with another experi-enced goaltender like himself – someone whose moti-vation was mainly to help a team out without needlessly exhausting himself – then it might be possi-ble. Jacques remembered that during the 1964-1965 season, when the League consisted of six much stronger teams, two veteran goalkeepers had shared the nets for the Toronto Maple Leafs: Johnny Bower, who was at least five years older than Jacques, and Terry Sawchuk. Together, they had even won the Vézina Trophy that year.

Jacques began to view the possibility more seri-ously; he was waiting for the right moment and a pro-posal that really suited him. Now, when reporters asked him about a comeback, he would answer, "Everyone in hockey has my phone number."

"Does that mean you're ready to strap on your leg pads?"

"I didn't say that. But *I am* ready to hear whatever people have to say to me. *Cercueil!* It doesn't hurt to listen!"

∞

In June 1968, the draft session took place at the Queen Elizabeth Hotel in Montreal, as usual. Jacques came to have lunch with a few of his former teammates and adversaries, but he couldn't attend the main event, as he had to go back to work. He had barely entered his office when he received a telephone call with some startling news.

"You've just been picked by the St. Louis Blues."

Jacques couldn't believe it: the Blues, the best team in the Western Conference, the team that had barely been edged out for the Stanley Cup by the Canadiens the previous spring! This was an interesting development, even more so because the Blues already had Glenn Hall, Jacques' long-time competitor for the Vézina Trophy – a seasoned veteran like he was, and one who had won the latest Conn Smythe Trophy for best player in the playoffs.

But even better than that, the Blues were managed by a man for whom Jacques had the highest degree of admiration and esteem: none other than Scotty Bowman. Bowman, like Jacques, was an intelligent hockey analyst. He had observed the effectiveness of Punch Imlach's system of having two veteran goalies alternating in the nets on a regular basis, giving their best without tiring themselves out, and without having to compete against each other for the number 1 position. An expert in defensive strategy, Bowman still remembered Jacques' impressive performance against the Russians. He knew that with Jacques Plante on his team, the Blues would have all the chances on their side to repeat their exploit of the previous season – in fact, he was convinced that they would do even better.

Scotty Bowman rarely showed poor judgment. Neither
did Jacques. Hockey was in his blood; he wanted to be
able to achieve the ambitions that he had put on hold.
He accepted the Blues' offer. For sharing the goaltending job with Glenn Hall, Jacques would earn the highest salary of his career, $35,000 for the season. He
wanted to be well prepared, and for that reason, he
underwent another operation, this time on his right
knee, which had still been giving him problems during
his Old-Timer games. His "old" body would be able to
catch up to him on the road of his dreams.

∞

The 1968-1969 edition of the St. Louis Blues was a
well-balanced mixture of seasoned veterans – players
whose glory days were over, but who could still outrank
their rivals as a team – and a few intense, young players. In the home zone were: Doug Harvey, who, for
more than a decade, had been considered the best
defenceman in the world; Jean-Guy Talbot, formerly of
the Canadiens; Noël Picard, who at thirty, had finally
reached the major league; and the Plager brothers,
Bob and Barclay. The forwards were: Red Berenson,
who had also played for the Canadiens and had established a record by scoring six times in a game against
the Philadelphia Flyers on November 7, 1968; Camille
Henry, the ex-poison of the Rangers; Ab McDonald,
Terry Crisp, Frank St. Marseille, and Gary Sabourin.
And behind all these formidable athletes, guarding the
fortress, were two legends: Glenn Hall and Jacques
Plante.

Scotty Bowman's solution was not identical to Punch Imlach's: it was actually a three-goalie system. When Jacques was on the ice, Glenn Hall would be in the press box, and vice-versa. The backup goaltender, either young Gary Edwards or Robbie Irons (they also alternated), would be available on the bench. The two younger goalies, although they practised with the team, did not face many pucks that season. The team's true goaltenders were Hall and Plante.

Proof of this came one evening when Glenn Hall was expelled from the game for having bawled out the referee who had credited a doubtful goal to the Rangers. Robbie Irons slid off the end of the bench to take his place between the goal posts. Jacques didn't hesitate for a second: he rushed to the dressing room, put on his uniform, and went to report to Bowman behind the bench. On a timely suggestion by Doug Harvey, Irons' ankle was "injured" by the first shot to come his way. He was immediately replaced by Jacques Plante – and the rest is history. The Rangers couldn't get the puck past Jacques that night, and the Blues won the game 3-1. In the crunch, the Blues ultimately placed their faith in their veteran goaltenders.

Jacques was far away from his family once again. But the atmosphere in St. Louis did not get him down like that of New York City or Baltimore. He wrote long daily letters, three or four pages each, to his wife Jacqueline; he had always enjoyed writing. He told her everything that happened to him during the day. He also amused himself by cooking – especially Italian food. Jacques kept his insatiable curiosity alive throughout his life, and his years away from hockey had brought him a greater maturity. Perhaps because there was less pressure on him, Jacques took life more calmly – a game at a time as far as his performance on the job went, and a year at a time as far as his long-term career plans were concerned.

In addition, the spirit that Blues' owner Syd Solomon III wanted to instill in the team harmonized with Jacques' own views. He soon became a friend of the Solomon family. It was understood that Jacques would never mind the nets for two games consecutively. The day after playing a game, more often than not, he was invited to go fishing with the team owner, to be able to fully relax. Solomon had also fixed up a clubhouse near the hotel where several of the players lived, a place where they could get together to talk, watch television, or play pool or ping-pong. Jacques was careful to keep himself in good condition. At thirty-nine years of age, an athlete has to watch for signs of deterioration, and for a man as conscientious as Jacques Plante was, exercises were a normal part of the daily routine.

Syd Solomon was a big-hearted man who thought of a thousand and one details to make his players happy – things that sports clubs rarely bother with. For example, on Jacques' fortieth birthday, the arena organist broke into "Happy Birthday to You" as soon as the goaltender skated onto the ice for that evening's game. Jacques was even more surprised when the fans began to sing, substituting "Jacques" for "You." Deeply touched by this kind gesture, the new quadragenarian showed his appreciation by playing a terrific game which ended by Blues tied with Rangers 2-2.

Solomon genuinely liked his players, and particularly admired his goaltenders. Hall and Plante rewarded him well for his trust in them. Each in turn handed in sparkling performances. The two old warriors got along like a house on fire and they obtained incredible results.

That year, an astonishing number of goals were scored in the NHL. Besides Bobby Hull's 58, several star forwards scored over 40 goals each, including Phil Esposito for the Bruins and Frank Mahovlich for the Red Wings, with 49 goals apiece. Even the veteran Gordie Howe, still powerful at forty-one years old, succeeded in scoring 44 times that season. The only club that didn't have a superior pointgetter was St. Louis. However, behind a rather slow but extremely experienced defence line, Jacques and Glenn blocked everything that came at them. The tandem won the Vézina Trophy that year, allowing 40 fewer goals than their closest rivals, the Rangers goaltenders.

The Blues had become the shutout kings of the NHL. Hall had posted 8, with a goals-against average of 2.17 in 40 games, while Jacques, having played 37 games, had an incredibly low goals-against average of 1.96, with 5 shutouts!

Along with these fantastic results, Jacques played on the Western Conference All-Star team, coached by Scotty Bowman. Together, they upheld the spirit of St. Louis by leading the team to a 3-3 tie with the powerful Eastern Conference All-Stars.

In the playoffs, the Blues had easily eliminated the Flyers, then the Kings, both times in only four games. However, in the final series, they were unable to mark even one victory over the Canadiens, who won their sixteenth Stanley Cup.

Jacques tended the net for the Blues in 10 playoff games, letting in only 14 goals. More significantly for his personal statistics, he chalked up his fourteenth shutout in a playoff series, beating the record set by Turk Broda, the former star goalie of the Toronto Maple Leafs.

Jacques had been right: there had been new heights to reach. He definitely entered a special category when he won his seventh Vézina Trophy, an all-time record in hockey. But besides earning that prestigious and unique title, he had proved that he was flexible enough to adapt to the new playing style that now dominated North American pro hockey. *Observation, analysis,* and *execution*: these three words could have constituted Jacques Plante's motto. The only word missing was *perfectionism*.

Of course, it was impossible to block every shot. Although the best teams in the NHL were still those of the Eastern Conference, the hockey played in the West was of a surprisingly high calibre. The following season, Jacques Plante and Glenn Hall were still at their posts in the Blues' net. Between the two of them, they allowed only 179 goals during the season, 9 more than Tony Esposito of the Chicago Black Hawks, who won the Vézina that year. Jacques' goals-against average was 2.19, with 5 shutouts added to his total.

In the season's first match between the Blues and the Big Bad Bruins, Fred Stanfield let fly a powerful shot from the tip of his stick-blade. Phil Esposito slapped the deflected puck straight into Jacques' mask. The goaltender collapsed, falling heavily onto the ice.

When he regained consciousness hours later at the Jewish Hospital of St. Louis, he heard a nurse saying, "Even if you were wearing your mask, you still had a serious concussion."

The mask...the mask...the word spun around in Jacques' head. His still-confused consciousness seized on the word, and with unexpected presence of mind, he retorted, "Maybe. But without the mask, you wouldn't be talking to me now. I'd be at the morgue."

Jacques was indomitable. Even flat on his back and unable to move his limbs, he still had to defend his ideas. However, the injury meant that Jacques' season was over – as well as his marvellous years with St. Louis.

For the third year running, the Blues were the Western Conference champions and went to the finals to lose the Stanley Cup – this time to the Boston Bruins, who had another kind of innovator in their ranks: the young Bobby Orr, the first defenceman to win the scoring championship. It was Orr's year, for besides having scored 120 goals, he won the Norris Trophy for best defenceman, the Hart Trophy for most valuable player, and the Conn Smythe Trophy for best player in the playoffs. While Jacques Plante had taught goalies that they could be effective out of the net, Bobby Orr had shown defencemen that if they skated fast enough, they could initiate plays that could completely change the pace of the game.

∞

At the end of the 1969-1970 season, Jacques went home to Laval-des-Rapides. The old warhorse could hold his head high and enjoy the satisfaction of a job well done. But, as usual, Jacques' duty to himself was not limited to simply excelling in his profession and resting on his laurels once the summer came. He threw himself into a demanding routine of physical activity. Along with twenty minutes of calisthenics, he worked out on an exercise cycle for ten minutes, three times a day. He also played tennis. But that was not the extent of his activities. Since he had first worn his mask ten years before, Jacques had never stopped upgrading the prototype to improve both the visual and protective aspects. His factory in Magog, in southeastern Quebec, was producing between 8,000 and 9,000 masks a year. He constantly received requests for technical advice from Sweden and other European countries, and from all parts of North America. Earlier that year, to provide greater protection for young goaltenders, he had adapted his "invention," integrating it with a hockey helmet. Soon after that, he handed over the running of production operations to his son, Michel.

In June of that year, at the annual draft session, Jacques was again taken by surprise: the Blues had sold him to the Toronto Maple Leafs. The Leafs, who had finished the previous season at the bottom of their division, wanted a good goaltending duo. They had decided on Bruce Gamble, a goalie of average talent, and Jacques Plante.

Several years afterwards, when a reporter asked Scotty Bowman what he considered the best transaction of his career, he replied, "The best deal I made was bringing Jacques Plante to St. Louis."

"And the worst?"

"It was when I let him go to Toronto."

Toronto was where Jacques had suffered his worst asthma attacks. Even though the Leafs' management had rented him a spacious apartment in the hope that he would not suffer respiratory distress, Jacques soon realized that his asthma was still active. Not only did he suffer from attacks, but he felt a continual constriction in his throat. He had frequent checkups at the hospital and underwent allergy tests. It was a stressful situation for Jacques, but he refused to give in. In trying to conserve his energy, he lost weight, going down to only seventy-seven kilograms. He led a hermit's existence, going to bed at 8:30 p.m. when the Leafs didn't have an evening game, and rising at 7:00 a.m. He read a lot, spent hours answering his fan mail, and wrote to his wife every day.

As soon as the practice sessions began, coach John McLellan took advantage of Jacques' vast knowledge of the game. He asked him to train the defence line which was made up of very young, inexperienced players. Jacques delighted in this challenge and buckled down to work with a will. During the games, he minded the net with great aplomb. He was pleased in February 1971, when the Leafs traded Bruce Gamble for a more talented goaltender, Bernie Parent.

Jacques had known Bernie for a long time. Years before, he had gone to see him play for Rosemont in the Montreal Metropolitan League. The young goaltender, who started in the NHL with the Bruins, then played for the Flyers, had always cited Jacques Plante as his idol. In return, Jacques was convinced that

Parent was destined to become one of the world's great goalies. Once again, time proved Jacques right. That year in Toronto, he viewed Bernie Parent as his protégé and successor. Later, Parent would be recognized as Jacques' spiritual heir.

Thanks to Jacques' performance, the Leafs finished the season in a respectable fourth place. Jacques was chosen for the second All-Star team. Toronto was eliminated early on in the playoffs – it was the first year that Ken Dryden tended goal for the Canadiens, who won the Stanley Cup.

At forty-three years of age, Jacques knew that his playing days were numbered. Since his debut in professional hockey, the great goaltender had profoundly influenced the sport. In 1972, he collaborated with veteran sports journalist Andy O'Brien to write *The Jacques Plante Story*, in which he recaptured the decisive moments of his life and career. Naturally, he contributed his views on the evolution of hockey technique in general, and on the individual styles of some of the exceptional players he had known.

Jacques still loved to talk, and he generously gave young hockey hopefuls the benefit of his experience. That summer at home, for the sixth year in a row, he taught his art at the École moderne de hockey, one of many hockey schools for young people that were sprouting up all over North America. He lent his enthusiastic support to these schools and freely revealed his professional secrets to aspiring goaltenders. He summed them up in ten fundamental principles. For Jacques Plante, a good goalie should:

1. be a good skater;
2. be a good stick-handler;
3. eliminate dangerous rebounds by bending the legs;
4. constantly watch the puck;
5. help teammates in the home zone by talking to them;
6. never move back into the net when an opponent comes in to shoot (it is better to move forward, even a few inches) and move horizontally across the net if an opponent cuts over in front of it;
7. bend over for blind shots from the blue-line and not stretch up on the toes;
8. place the blade of the stick onto the ice when an opponent shoots during a scrum in front of the net;
9. come out of the net to stop a long bouncing shot on the first bounce;
10. hit the puck into the corner instead of diving onto it during a goal-mouth scrum.

Jacques was much in demand as a lecturer and special guest at social and sports events, where he never hesitated to express his original ideas. He felt that minor league hockey focused too much on winning games, and that for players under the age of ten, hockey ought to be mainly recreational instead of competitive – an activity in which young people could learn their skills without having to endure the gruelling criticism that prevails in organized hockey.

Jacques' reputation as an exceptional communicator spread; he was even solicited by groups outside the continent. In the spring of 1972, the Swedish Hockey Federation, on a suggestion by retired player Billy Harris, asked Jacques to give some lessons to its goaltenders. At first, he declined, having too many engagements at home, but the Swedes continued to press him. Finally, he offered them one summer weekend, and thus, at the end of July, he travelled to Lexsand, 250 kilometres from Stockholm, to give pointers on the profession of which, by his verve and experience, he was the uncontested world master.

His pupils in Lexsand included the eight best goalies in the country, as well as about twenty trainer/coaches of the high-calibre teams of the Swedish National League. The Plante method was a complete revelation to these neophytes who, before that, had followed the dull, pragmatic instructions given in their Czechoslovakian goaltending manuals. Jacques did not limit his approach to the usual basic puck-stopping techniques: he mainly wanted to teach them to think, and to learn about playing strategies. He also taught them the art of roving from the net, and how to predict what would happen in certain circumstances – in short, he taught them how to use their intelligence and imagination. That was the precious gift that only Jacques Plante, among all the hockey greats of the time, could have given them.

Jacques defined three basic goaltending styles: the butterfly, or V-position to protect the lower half of the net using the full breadth of the leg pads; the classic style of standing upright, covering the corners, and making decisions according to the principles of play;

and, finally, the "Worsley" style of plunging to the right or left in anticipation of the shots.

Jacques had a wonderful sense of humour and adored teaching, since it required him to look at all the aspects of his profession to be able to pass on his knowledge effectively. In the same year, he wrote *Goaltending*, published by Collier-Macmillan of Canada (the French-language version, *Devant le filet*, was published by Éditions de l'Homme). In the foreword, Jacques made these pertinent remarks:

> A goalie depends so much on his teammates' playing that at times it gets on his nerves and he loses his temper. Goalkeepers are a breed apart because of the work they do and because no one else can understand what they go through before and during a game. After the game, they often have to explain what happened on many goals. Most of the time they accept the blame, because it is their job to stop the puck, but when they point out another player's error, they are called poor losers trying to find excuses for their mistake.
>
> To succeed, goalies have to have strong willpower, pride in their work, a lot of ability – more than any other player – good judgment, steel nerves, and a high degree of resistance to endure all the injuries they suffer during the course of a season....
>
> If you look at me today, you'll notice a lot of grey hair, which is often the sign of

wisdom. Maybe that's true in my case. Certainly, it took long enough for me to get where I am, and I don't think I could have done any better than I did....

Remember that goalkeeping is an art. To master it, you have to continuously adjust your style to conserve energy, remain strong until the end of each game, and consequently play better. You have to read, observe, listen, question, and practise every chance you get.

All my life, I learned through my mistakes because no one could help me. You don't have that problem. But you'll discover that goalies aren't made in a day. You have to grow up, mature, and suffer a multitude of setbacks and defeats before you can become a great goalie. And even then, the work doesn't stop.

Humbly then, in the autumn of 1972, Jacques Plante offered the public the first goaltender's bible. No one else could have done it.

∞

The summer of 1972 was one of the worst periods ever for professional hockey. After grafting two new teams to its roster two years earlier – the Vancouver Canucks and the Buffalo Sabres – the NHL added a further duo of rookie teams to the scoreboard: the Atlanta Flames and the New York Islanders. This additional expansion diluted the talent even further, and the situation was exacerbated by the formation of a whole new league, the World Hockey Association (WHA).

To become established in pro hockey and to attract fans, the WHA set up teams in twelve North American cities and immediately set out to siphon off the most promising talent from the NHL – which had monopolized professional hockey until then – by contracting the best young players, that is, those who were willing to take the risk of leaping into the unknown. Thus, from one day to the next, the face of the game was completely transformed. Bobby Hull, who had scored 604 goals in 13 seasons for Chicago, signed a million-dollar contract with the Winnipeg Jets of the WHA. All of a sudden, every player with the least bit of talent was offered a choice between the two leagues. Several well-known players went over to the WHA, including goaltenders Gerry Cheevers and Bernie Parent, defenceman Jean-Claude Tremblay, and forwards Dave Keon, Johnny McKenzie, and Frank Mahovlich. The following year, even the great Gordie Howe defected to the Houston Aeros, mainly because he wanted to play with his sons, Marty and Mark – a first-ever in the history of the sport. In one fell swoop, the geography, but especially the economics of hockey were turned upside-down. Things were not going well for the NHL, but there was still worse to come in April of the same year.

The League's prestige was irrevocably tarnished by a highly publicized event that was promoted as "the series of the century" but should have been nicknamed "the red menace." Star NHL players from Canada were grouped into a supposedly invincible team that would take on a elite team from the U.S.S.R.

Jacques Plante, understandably, had been familiar with Soviet hockey for years, assiduously following its progress. For this reason, Radio-Canada, the French-language network of Canada's national broadcasting company, asked Jacques to act as an on-air analyst during the televised game. North American hockey fans presumed that the Soviets, even if they had dominated world amateur hockey for years, would be wiped off the ice by real NHL pros. The players themselves did not view the Soviets as serious competitors. The only voices that dared to dissent from majority opinion were those of Michel Blanchard, sports columnist for *La Presse*... and that experienced observer, Jacques Plante.

Minutes before the first game of the series, played at the Montreal Forum, Jacques entered the visiting team's dressing room, accompanied by an interpreter. Vladislav Tretyak, the young goaltender whose extraordinary talent had not yet been revealed to North American hockey fans, was astonished to see the legendary goalie walking towards him. Jacques, always the conscientious teacher, proceeded to explain to Tretyak how to outplay Mahovlich, Esposito, Cournoyer, and Henderson!

Tretyak, still in shock, had no time to reply. Jacques bid farewell to the Russian players and left. The young goaltender wondered why the former Habs goalie had graced him by this special honour...could it be that Jacques pitied him, given the opponents' attitude that they were going to crush the Soviet team? In any case, Tretyak took Jacques' advice to heart, and on the ice, he showed that he was up to the standard of any NHL goalie.

On the air, during the breaks between periods, Jacques used the blackboard to point out the strategies that the Soviet coach was deploying against the Canadian attack. The Team Canada players, on the other hand, had not bothered to analyse this aspect: they had always viewed the Soviets as good players, but of minor-league calibre compared to the NHL pros. It was a hard pill to swallow when the very first game resulted in a humiliating defeat for Canada. The plain fact was that Europeans, spearheaded by the Soviets, knew how to play hockey and could now beat the North Americans at their own game.

It took the members of Team Canada a long time to come to grips with this reality, but they finally managed to win the series, thanks to Paul Henderson's goal during the final minute of play in the decisive last game.

In the fall of 1972, pro hockey had difficulty digesting the double-whammy of the economics lesson from the WHA and the lesson in hockey skills from the U.S.S.R. Players and managers were clearly shaken. In Toronto, Jacques imperturbably continued tending net with his usual skill and dedication. A rumour was circulating that the WHA Quebec City Nordiques had made him an interesting offer to coach the team the following season, but if there was any truth in it, Jacques himself kept mum.

On Friday March 2, 1973, Jacques Plante was traded to the Boston Bruins, who had been desperately looking for a top-level goalkeeper since Gerry Cheevers' defection to the WHA. They wanted a goaltender who would give them a run at the Stanley Cup.

The Bruins paid dearly in the bargain, sacrificing the first-round draft pick for the following season to the Maple Leafs.

In his new uniform, Jacques, who knew that the Bruins had a good chance of sweeping the honours that year, acquitted himself honourably, allowing 16 goals in 8 games and posting 2 shutouts. In the playoffs, however, he let in 10 goals in 2 games, and was replaced.

According to his contract, he was slated to play another season in the NHL with the Bruins. But after the finals, Jacques remained at the Hotel Sonesta in Boston to tie up his promotional activities, and on April 12, 1973, a bomb detonated: Jacques Plante had accepted a ten-year million-dollar contract as general manager and coach of the Quebec Nordiques.

This electrifying news spread like a trail of gunpowder and was on the front pages of the sports sections of all the newspapers in North America the next morning.

Overtime

The Man Who Carried a
Filing Cabinet in His Head

Throughout his career, Jacques Plante writes hockey columns
for several newspapers and magazines.

Portland, Maine, March 25, 1978.

J acques Plante, former star NHL goaltender, spent much of the spring season here, in a room at the Holiday Inn. This room was his refuge. How many hotels rooms, all over North America, had he known? In how many hotel rooms had he run through a game in his mind, just after playing it? How many times had he rehashed and reconsidered his career moves in this setting? Jacques had travelled a lot, and by that token, had spread himself thin. The hotel room had become the symbol of his solitude – the solitude of the thinker, as well as the unbearable solitude of homesickness and boredom. The goaltender had been forced to endure the necessary separation from his loved ones: for years, with the Royals and especially with the Canadiens, he had been the loner in the group, far from his young family. But the team had always returned home, and Montreal had remained his anchor of stability. The feeling of empty restlessness, of being a wanderer, had first come upon him when he had been traded to New York.

The time and place mentioned in connection with this stage of Jacques' life story are arbitrary, although the heading of Portland appears frequently in the long letters he wrote during this period – indefatigably – daily, or even twice a day. It could just as well have bcon January 29, 1979, or December 11, 1980, at the Hilton Hotel in Philadelphia.

In his room, Jacques filled page after page; he had always loved to write.

For many years, of course, the main subject of his writing had been hockey. In 1957, in the middle of his best years with the Habs, he had written a hockey column for *La Voix de Shawinigan*, as if he wanted to share some of his glory with the town where he grew up. Later, in New York City, perhaps as a way to stay connected to his roots, he sent a weekly column to *Le Samedi* (later called *Le Nouveau Samedi*). At the same time, he wrote for *Sports* magazine. Jacques was a consistently observant commentator who paid attention to details; he described what lay behind the athletes' performances – their diets, their training programs, their practice schedules – along with a dose of gossip about the players' attitudes, occasionally mixed with his own particular philosophy of sports. His columns invariably contained pertinent examples that revealed a deep understanding of the nature of spectator sports, and of the people who strive to stand out in this area of human endeavour. He never refused when he was asked to submit a column: writing had been such a pleasure for him since his school days.

Writing is also the medium of solitary people who want to communicate, to reach others on a level beyond banal small talk. Now, in Portland, he found himself in the familiar situation once again, although this time, his solitary vigil took the form of an intimate dialogue. During the last years of his life, Jacques found another means of expression – as a lover.

∞

Portland, March 25, 1978; it could have been any other day or place. After leaving active play three years earlier, Jacques was often called upon to help other goaltenders. He had become a kind of therapist for them. It was known throughout the hockey world that Jacques Plante could accurately analyse a goaltender's skills and apply the appropriate corrections and improvements to them, taking their different opponents' styles into account in the process. He had a reputation as a human filing system, a walking repository of statistical analysis. Along with his amazing skill on the ice in his prime, these attributes explain why Jacques continued to travel all over the continent.

Jacques had been the first influential hockey guru to recommend more than one coach per team: one supervising the goaltender and the defencemen, and the other directing the forwards. Hockey was evolving rapidly, and this system was now being used more frequently. Yes, there had been some improvements to the game, but in other aspects, it had changed for the worse. Jacques' unfortunate sojourn in Quebec City was proof of this. Ever afterwards, he was unable to erase that dreadful year from his memory.

∞

The year with the Nordiques.

Given Jacques Plante's reputation as a tightwad, people might have been forgiven for presuming that he, like some other players who ended up behind the bench, was heading to Quebec City mostly for the money. In fact, several other factors had motivated his decision.

"My return to Quebec has nothing to do with money," he firmly declared. "I'm just happy to be going back to my native province."

Jacques had never hidden his distaste for big cities. In all the large urban centres where his career had taken him, he had experienced varying degrees of respiratory distress. His asthma was not the sole cause of it. Even more than his physical and medical condition, his discomfort was due to the feeling of incompleteness that he experienced whenever he was far from home. Back in Quebec, as he said himself, he could finally sleep in peace.

Disappointed by his results with Boston in the 1973 playoffs, Jacques had been looking for a career change in any case, and it had been provided by the offer from Quebec City.

On December 13, 1970, he had met a young Swiss woman, Raymonde Udrisard. She had come to work at Man and his World, an offshoot of the Montreal World's Fair of 1967, and had stayed in Canada. She had gradually taken a larger and larger place in Jacques' life, and they had begun living together. This had certainly been a reason for Jacques' desire to end his nomadic existence. But his overriding motivation had been, as usual, his love of hockey: he knew the game as well or better than anyone else, and he was ready to meet the challenge of using this knowledge in a new way.

In that spring of re-evaluation in the aftermath of his disappointing time with the Bruins, Jacques was well aware that his life would change radically if he accepted the job of manager and coach of the Nordiques. However, in spite of all his experience and acumen, for the first time since hockey had become the focal point of his world, Jacques misjudged his new role, which had nothing to do with stopping pucks. In fact, he plunged into the worst nightmare of his life, and would only emerge from it badly demoralized.

As always, with Jacques Plante, nothing happened in a commonplace manner; with him, the ordinary took on an inspired, prodigal aspect. With his active, innovative mind, strong personality, and deep knowledge, Jacques knew exactly what he wanted to accomplish. But did he have the ability to take his players, the club owners, reporters, and fans in the same direction? When he tended net, he had been the target of bitter criticism – the common fate of innovators. Now, in his double role of manager and coach, he had to play a lone hand once again. He had to evaluate and select his players, pay them, and convince them to play well for him. In other words, he had to ask the players to justify his choices.

As a team member, Jacques had always been able to counter the criticism levelled at his unconventional opinions and his outspoken comments by the evidence of his skill. Because he was directly in the line of fire and shouted out instructions while defending the nets, Jacques' orders were accepted unquestioningly by the other players, who had only to look to his example – and as a player, he had succeeded magnificently. Working behind the bench, however, requires a completely different kind of talent. Jacques quickly learned that a manager can bring together the best possible combination of players, and a coach can devise the best strategies in the world, but neither of them have skates on their feet nor sticks in their hands. They can issue all the forceful orders that they like and provide the most expert advice, but this doesn't necessarily produce the desired results on the ice. And in major league professional sports, a manager's decisions have got to lead to victories right from the start, especially at a time when the sport itself is undergoing rapid changes.

Jacques began by going after the big guns. He wanted to contract Jean Béliveau, who had once been the adored star player of the Quebec City Aces, but "Big Bill" preferred his peaceful retirement. Next, Jacques tried to obtain Guy Lafleur, a more recent hockey idol, but the Blond Demon chose to play for the Canadiens. Jacques' efforts to recruit Réjean Houle and Serge Bernier fared better, and the two forwards joined the Nordiques in their first foray into the WHA. Together with defenceman Jean-Claude Tremblay, they formed a strong nucleus of francophone talent – but one that, unfortunately, did not prove strong enough to shake the other teams in the new system.

At the same time, Jacques was writing a weekly column in a local paper, *À-propos*, and succeeded in putting several reporters up in arms against him, which did not help the team's morale. In spite of his astonishing amount of knowledge, Jacques was too much of a dreamer to succeed as a coach in pro hockey. The high-pressure job was a thousand miles away from the training camps, where eager young goaltenders listened respectfully to an expert's pointers on improving their play. Coaching a professional team in 1973-74 was more a matter of motivating overpaid players – a task that sometimes seemed to require the strength of Atlas, even if the coach knew that he was not expected to carry the whole team on his shoulders.

The team that Jacques had promised to take to the playoffs faltered lamentably, and at the end of the season, Jacques was induced to resign. Claude Larochelle reported Jacques' departure in Quebec City's main daily newspaper, *Le Soleil*, on May 2, 1974:

PLANTE HANDS IN HIS RESIGNATION
The news is surprising, to say the least. People who know Jacques Plante intimately assured me that he would hang on to his contract until the end, and that the shareholders who wanted to show him the door would have a long struggle on their hands to get rid of him....

The news is stupefying at first glance. But if we look closer, we understand that Plante, a man who has always been affable and reasonable until the end had to admit the facts – the facts that were obvious to everyone who was following his progress with any attention. A superb goaltender and a refined game analyst, he wasn't able to transpose onto the ice what he could express so well in words. He didn't have what it takes to be a manager. He was certainly aware that the shareholders' case against him was getting more serious and more irrefutable every day.

Jacques' response to this unpleasant situation was to go back onto the ice for a comeback, as he had done in the past. Four days after his official resignation from his duties with the Quebec Nordiques, the Edmonton Oilers announced that they were contracting Jacques Plante – as goalie! At forty-five, revolted by his ordeal behind the bench, Jacques longed to put on his mask and leg pads and return to his first love: goaltending.

The best that can be said about the Oilers' 1974-1975 season is that Jacques was consoled after the fiasco with the Nordiques by tending goal. But it was slight consolation: Jacques shared the job with Chris Worthy, and the team, although strong defensively, was weak in offensive play. The Oilers finished in last place in the Canadian division of the WHA and did not reach the playoffs.

The following autumn, Jacques reported to the Oilers' training camp. But just before the beginning of the season, he learned of the death of his younger son. Jacques hung up his skates for good.

At forty-nine years of age, Jacques Plante, who had lived through more difficult situations than most hockey players, was coaching the fledgling goaltenders of the Maine Mariners, a Philadelphia Flyers' farm club in the American League. They were, in succession: Rick Sainte-Croix, Phil Myre, Pete Peeters, Bob Froese, and the Swede, Pelle Lindberg. More than ever before, Jacques was a hotly sought-after consultant in his area of expertise, and he continued to practise this activity for the rest of his life. Most of that period was spent within the Flyers' organization, but he also worked with the Canadiens in 1984-1985, and with the St. Louis Blues.

Besides teaching their potential goaltenders, Jacques occasionally went to watch games played by the adversaries of the Flyers. This was the team that had proved him a liar after he had confidently said in 1967 that the new expansion teams would have to play for ten years before winning the Stanley Cup: the Flyers, partly because of their rough playing style, won the prestigious trophy in both 1974 and 1975, just seven years after their inception. Their number 1 goaltender, Bernie Parent – Jacques' acolyte – had become the best goalie in the NHL.

When he wasn't in a hotel room or in an arena, Jacques spent most of his time on airplanes between Boston, New York, and Pittsburgh. He was observing, taking notes, and writing columns. He travelled with his life in his suitcase, his heart full. Although hotel rooms all look alike, he infused them with his love. This is why his letters to Raymonde were so intense and spontaneous.

His pen moved across the page, but he could not write fast enough to express all he felt for her. Jacques himself admitted that he was a fool in love. When they were miles apart, he constantly wrote her passionate letters, declaring that he was the happiest man on earth. Writing was Jacques' preferred means to bridge the distance between himself and his beloved.

He would often stare at the wall of his room and visualize Raymonde standing in front of him, coming to life. He kept a photograph of her next to his bed, to feel close to her when he turned off the lamp to go to sleep, and so that her smile would be the first thing he saw when he opened his eyes in the morning. He carried three other pictures of her in his wallet. His favourite one was a snapshot taken during their trip to Lake Louise; it was a souvenir of a happy break that had briefly transported him far from his problems with the Nordiques, and had marked the beginning of their new life together.

In his letters, Jacques tenderly evoked the times they had shared, the affection that had grown between them, in Toronto and Boston, Quebec City and Edmonton, until they finally settled down in Switzerland. He recalled the first days of their romance, when he, the NHL star, would go to wait for her after work, like a bashful young man at the stage door. But mostly, he shared the events of his day with his beloved, as if she were with him wherever he went.

They are love letters, to be sure, but they also constitute a vibrant tribute to a woman who had taught him to share his innermost thoughts, and to appreciate the people he worked with. From Raymonde, Jacques had learned the patience necessary to teach aspiring goaltenders how to best develop their skills.

He succeeded in exorcising his loneliness and gave it meaning. He wrote to Raymonde twice a day, attentive to the anniversary of every occasion they had shared, particularly the date of their meeting.

In the same way that he gave all he had in his professional life, Jacques was a passionate lover. He was a forthright, wholehearted man. He was so completely wrapped up in the relationship that sometimes, his heart would beat so hard that he thought it would burst from his chest. It tortured him to be separated from the woman he loved, for whom he composed delicate poetry. Jacques' work still obliged him to spend much of his time in distant cities, but his thoughts no longer centered on the ice; he expressed his great happiness on paper.

∞

The *Canadien errant* – the homesick native son of the old French Canadian folk-song – was still a wanderer, but he was no longer an unwilling exile. He cut the ties that bound him to his country. In 1979, he closed the mask factory in Magog that he had started in 1970. He moved to Sierre, a town in the Swiss Alps, with Raymonde.

Nonetheless, in Canada, Jacques remained a much-appreciated broadcast analyst whenever there were special hockey events. To give just one example, Jacques was the analyst for the TVA broadcasts of the Canada Cup series in which Team Canada faced the best teams in the world. He was the most articulate of all the French-speaking athletes who had played this sport. It was not just his mastery of language (he now expressed himself as well in English as in French): people listened to Jacques Plante because they found what he said pertinent and interesting. His comments revealed a truly contemporary grasp of hockey.

This particular *Canadien errant* never completely stopped travelling. But in Sierre, his new home, the much scarred warrior finally took his rest. He found time to paint. He learned German. He skied and played tennis with Raymonde. A peaceable man, Jacques' pleasures were simple; his friends were Charlie the restaurant owner, Émile the winegrower, and Zizi the innkeeper. From time to time, he would give a little coaching advice to the city's hockey club. Hockey was still in his blood.

When he was summoned by the North American hockey world during the season, Jacques would pack his bags again. He and Raymonde would fly to Florida where she would sunbathe at the home of friends while Jacques prepared to consult his extraordinary mental filing system.

∞

Jacques Plante no longer wore his skates nor his heavy leg pads; he no longer set his wide-ended stick firmly on the ice; he no longer wore his mask – except, of course, when he gave lessons to young goalies. His fame continued to spread nevertheless. His name was already written in gold in the annals of sport. He had shone so brightly on the ice and had given so much to this spectacular sport that hockey rendered him its highest tribute.

On July 13, 1978, Jacques Plante was inducted into the Hockey Hall of Fame, in the company of Marcel Pronovost and Andy Bathgate. On September 13, 1978, he and Raymonde were the guests of honour at the Hall of Fame presentation dinner. Frank Selke, his first pro manager, delivered the main speech of the evening and

spoke glowingly of the goaltender's remarkable achievements. It was the crowning moment of Jacques' career,
the accomplishment of a lifetime, and the realization of
a hockey player's greatest hopes.

Seven years later, at a gala event at the Montreal
Forum, he was elected a member of the Habs all-time
dream team by popular vote. This was perhaps the
greatest of all honours from Jacques' point of view, as
the contenders included Bill Durnan, the man whom
Jacques had admired so much when he first trained
with the Canadians, and Ken Dryden, whose exploits
had brightened the end of the 1960s. But the public
had remembered Jacques Plante over all of them. He
was their choice for number 1 goaltender of the best
team of all time. On January 12, 1985, he appeared on
centre ice with the living legends he had revered:
defencemen Doug Harvey and Larry Robinson, centre
Jean Béliveau, left-winger Dickie Moore, right-winger
Maurice Richard, and coach Toe Blake. But wasn't he
himself part of the legend?

In January 1986, Jacques resumed his work as a hockey
consultant. He went to St. Louis to help goaltenders
Greg Millen and Rick Wamsley, who had played for the
Habs. One day when they were having lunch together,
coach Jacques Demers noticed that Jacques hardly ate
anything at all. He mentioned the fact to Dr. Probstein,
the Blues' physician, who examined Jacques and found
that he had lost seven kilograms in only a few weeks'
time.

Jacques was sent back to Switzerland, where he was diagnosed with stomach cancer. The disease had progressed to a point of no return. Jacques Plante died in Geneva on February 27, 1986, at 5:25 a.m. He was fifty-seven years old. The sports world was in shock, as the news of his disease had not been released to the media until his last days. Jacques had not wanted it to be divulged at all – he hated to be the source of trouble or worry for other people. The funeral took place in Sierre, and he was buried there. Jean-Claude Tremblay and Jean Béliveau attended on behalf of the Canadiens.

On March 11th, a memorial service was held at the Church of the Immaculate Conception in Montreal. Jacques' first wife, Jacqueline, his son, Michel, and numerous hockey personalities were present.

The officials of the Swiss National Hockey League announced the creation of the Jacques Plante Trophy, the equivalent of the Vézina Trophy for best goaltender of the year. Other honours continued to be bestowed on Jacques posthumously: he was inducted into the Quebec Pantheon of Sports Heroes on September 23, 1994, and on October 7, 1995, the Montreal Canadiens Hockey Club honoured him by retiring the uniform marked with the number 1 – Jacques' number when he had played for the Habs. In the year 2000, Canada Post dedicated a series of stamps to the greatest hockey players of the past century: the five selected were Maurice Richard, Doug Harvey, Gordie Howe, Bobby Hull, and Jacques Plante.

Certainly, these are valid ways to highlight the achievements of an extraordinary character in hockey history. But it is on the ice every night, on every hockey rink in the world, that the memory of an innovator of the likes of Jacques Plante is reborn – every time that commentators or coaches discuss a goaltender's ability to handle the puck outside the net, and every time a mask saves a goaltender from injury.

As long as the game is played, Jacques Plante's name will live on.

Jacques Plante and his son Michel, five years old.

Jacques Plante: Career Statistics

Season	Team	REGULAR SEASON				PLAYOFFS			
		GP	GA	S	AV	GP	GA	S	AV
1952-1953	Montreal	3	4	0	1.33	4	7	1	1.75
1953-1954	Montreal	17	27	5	1.59	8	15	2	1.88
1954-1955	Montreal	52	110	5	2.12	12	31	1	2.58
1955-1956	Montreal	64	119	7	1.86	10	18	2	1.80
1956-1957	Montreal	61	123	9	2.02	10	18	1	1.80
1957-1958	Montreal	57	119	9	2.09	10	20	1	2.00
1958-1959	Montreal	67	144	9	2.15	11	28	0	2.55
1959-1960	Montreal	69	175	3	2.54	8	11	3	1.38
1960-1961	Montreal	40	112	2	2.80	6	16	0	2.67
1961-1962	Montreal	70	166	4	2.37	6	19	0	3.17
1962-1963	Montreal	56	138	5	2.46	5	14	0	2.80
1963-1964	New York	65	220	3	3.38				
1964-1965	New York	33	109	2	3.30				
1968-1969	St. Louis	37	70	5	1.96	10	14	3	1.43
1969-1970	St. Louis	32	67	5	2.19	6	8	1	1.48
1970-1971	Toronto	40	73	4	1.88	3	7	0	3.13
1971-1972	Toronto	34	86	2	2.63	1	5	0	5.00
1972-1973	Toronto	32	87	1	3.04				
	Boston	8	16	2	2.00	2	10	0	5.00
(1974-1975	Edmonton	40	88	1	3.32)				
	(WHA)								
TOTALS,	NHL	837	1965	82	2.38	112	241	15	2.17

GP: Games played
GA: Goals against
S: Shutout achieved
AV: Goals-against average

Chronology of Jacques Plante (1929-1986)

Compiled by Michèle Vanasse

PLANTE AND THE WORLD OF SPORTS

CANADA AND THE WORLD

1910
The Montreal Canadiens, founded the previous year by J. Ambrose O'Brien, inaugurate the first season of the National Hockey Association (later the NHL).

Debut of goaltending great, Georges Vézina.

1917-1918
The National Hockey League (NHL) is inaugurated. On February 18th, Georges Vézina achieves the first shutout in NHL history.

1910
In Great Britain, King Edward VII is succeeded by George V.

1918
End of World War I; Canada has fought with the Allies against Germany, Austria, and Italy.

The deadly Spanish flu epidemic ravages the world, killing about 50,000 Canadians; some Quebec villages are exterminated by the disease.

Jacques Plante

1926-1927 season
The Vézina Trophy is established; it will be awarded to the NHL goalie who allows the lowest number of goals in the regular hockey season.

1929
Jacques Plante is born on January 17 on a farm near Mont Carmel in the Mauricie region of Quebec. He is the eldest son of Xavier Plante and Palma Brière. Soon after Jacques' birth, the family moves to Shawinigan Falls, where Xavier works for the Aluminum Company of Canada.

1929
Black Thursday on Wall Street on October 24; the American stock market collapses and the Great Depression (1929-1939) begins.

The prohibition of alcoholic beverages in the U.S. means profitable times for Canada-U.S. liquor smugglers. The gangster era in North America is at its height.

1932
At three, Jacques Plante begins to play hockey, skateless, using a goalie's stick made by his father, and tennis balls instead of pucks.

Sonja Henie of Norway wins three gold medals for figure skating at the Winter Olympic Games in Lake Placid, N.Y.

1932
In Canada, two new political parties arise in response to hard times: the socialist CCF (Co-operative Commonwealth Federation, forerunner of the New Democratic Party) led by James Woodsworth, and the Social Credit Party, founded by William Aberhart.

1934
At five, Jacques Plante breaks his wrist in a playground accident. The bones fail to heal properly, resulting in a handicap that moulds Plante's goalkeeping style, obliging him to use his body for blocking high shots.

1934
Adolf Hitler, leader of the totalitarian National Socialist, or Nazi Party, becomes absolute ruler of the German army and the government. Nazi repression of democrats, Jews, and Marxists intensifies.

The Dionne Quintuplets are born in northern Ontario.

PLANTE AND THE WORLD OF SPORTS

Left-winger Aurèle Joliat of the Canadiens wins the Hart Trophy for most valuable player.

The Masters Tournament in Atlanta, Georgia is founded by golf pro Walter Hagen.

Hank Greenberg is batting .333 for the Detroit Tigers.

1936
Jacques Plante enters primary school in Shawinigan. He receives his first real goalie's stick. He learns knitting – which becomes a lifelong pastime, an unusual one for a sports idol.

The Canadian Football League (CFL) is founded.

At the Berlin Summer Olympics, Black American athlete Jesse Owen sweeps the gold medals in track and field. Canada's gold is won by Frank Amyot in kayaking.

Sonja Henie again sweeps the gold medals in figure skating at the Winter Olympics in Garmisch.

1937
Montreal Canadiens great, Howie Morenz, dies from complications after his leg is broken in a game.

Boxer Joe Louis becomes world heavyweight champion, a title he will hold for twelve years.

CANADA AND THE WORLD

In Montreal, Mayor Camilien Houde opens the Jacques Cartier Bridge on the 400th anniversary of Cartier's arrival in Canada.

1936
In the Quebec elections, Maurice Duplessis leads the Union Nationale party to victory.

The Canadian Broadcasting Corporation is established.

In France, socialist party leader Léon Blum creates the Front populaire.

Hitler's Nazi Germany and Mussolini's Fascist Italy form an alliance.

Civil War begins in Spain between the Republicans and the extreme right/fascists under General Francisco Franco.

1937
In Great Britain, George VI is crowned king.

The civilian population of the Spanish town of Guernica is mercilessly bombed by the German air force. Pablo Picasso represents the tragedy in his best-known painting,

Jacques Plante

| PLANTE AND THE WORLD OF SPORTS | CANADA AND THE WORLD |

PLANTE AND THE WORLD OF SPORTS	CANADA AND THE WORLD
	Guernica, shown that same year at the Paris World Fair.
1938 American Don Budge makes a grand slam, winning four of the world's most prestigious tennis tournaments.	**1938** The Munich agreement, signed by Germany, Italy, Great Britain, and France, allows the Nazis to annex Czechoslovakian territory where a German-speaking majority lives.
1939 Hector "Toe" Blake wins the NHL scoring championship and the Hart Trophy for most valuable player. Because of the war, the Olympic Games are suspended until 1948. In the United States, a baseball game is televised for the first time.	**1939** World War II begins when Hitler invades Poland; England, France, and Canada declare war on Germany. The United States remains neutral while providing arms to Hitler's adversaries. In Quebec, Adelard Godbout of the Liberals is returned to the Premier's office. The Spanish Civil War ends in victory for Franco.
1941 At age twelve, Jacques Plante begins to play organized hockey as number 1 goalie for his school team of seventeen- and eighteen-year-olds. Hockey players are criticized by the public for being exempted from war service and from closed border rules between the U.S. and Canada. Joe DiMaggio sets a record by hitting base hits or better in 56 consecutive games.	**1941** The attack on Pearl Harbor brings the United States into the war against the Japanese and their allies, Germany and Italy. The U.S.S.R. declares war against Germany. Canada under Mackenzie King declares war on Japan without waiting for U.S. or British lead. As part of air-raid preparations, dusk-to-dawn blackouts are observed in Western Canada.

PLANTE AND THE WORLD OF SPORTS	CANADA AND THE WORLD
	Wartime price control begins in Canada.
1942	**1942**
Maurice "The Rocket" Richard debuts with the Canadiens under coach Dick Irvin Senior.	A majority of Canadians vote for wartime conscription in a plebiscite although the opposite result is obtained in the province of Quebec.
French boxer Marcel Cerdan becomes European middleweight champion.	
1944	**1944**
Jacques Plante plays in nets for four teams in four different categories: midget, juvenile, junior, and intermediate. He also plays for a Shawinigan factory team, earning fifty cents a game.	Maurice Duplessis of the Union Nationale party is returned to power in Quebec after five years on the opposition bench.
	The Allies land in Normandy on June 6th.
1945	**1945**
Rocket Richard shatters Joe Malone's 1917 record of 44 goals in one season by marking his 45th goal against the Toronto Maple Leafs. He becomes the first player to score 50 goals in 50 games.	In the U.S., President Roosevelt dies in office, and is replaced by Harry Truman.
	The atomic bomb is dropped on Hiroshima by the Americans; the Japanese surrender and the Allied victory in Europe ends World War II.
	The United Nations (UN) Organization is founded to keep world peace and to protect human rights.
1946	**1946**
Clarence Campbell becomes NHL president, and Frank Selke is named general manager of the Montreal Canadiens.	British Prime Minister Winston Churchill refers to the countries under Soviet domination as "the iron curtain countries."

Jacques Plante

PLANTE AND THE WORLD OF SPORTS	CANADA AND THE WORLD
The Montreal Alouettes of the CFL come into being.	
Jackie Robinson, the first black player in professional baseball, is a member of the Montreal Royals, an International League team.	
1947	**1947**
Jacques Plante graduates from high school and works as an office clerk in a Shawinigan factory. He refuses offers from the Providence Reds and from the Junior Canadiens, in favour of one from the Quebec Citadels. He begins to show his characteristic style of roaming beyond the goal crease, galvanizing the crowds.	Canada joins the UN. Great Britain grants independence to strife-torn India, which is partitioned into India and Pakistan. The U.S. Truman Doctrine aims to create a bulwark against communism in Europe by providing aid.
Jackie Robinson signs with a major league baseball team.	Under Walter Gordon, price controls are still in effect in Canada.
1948	**1948**
The Citadels, largely due to Jacques Plante's exploits, beat the Junior Canadiens in the finals.	Louis St. Laurent of the Liberal party becomes prime minister of Canada.
Plante is named best player of the year by the Shawinigan Softball League.	The United States adopts the Marshall Plan for European reconstruction.
Marcel Cerdan wins the world middleweight title.	Palestine is partitioned and the State of Israel comes into existence.
Figure skater Barbara Ann Scott of Ottawa wins the world championship and the gold medal at the St. Moritz Winter Olympics.	

PLANTE AND THE WORLD OF SPORTS	CANADA AND THE WORLD
1949	**1949**
Jacques Plante marries Jacqueline Gagné on April 30th.	Canada becomes a member of the North Atlantic Treaty Organization (NATO) with its mandate of defending the free world.
Plante plays for the Montreal Royals of the Quebec Senior League, but practises daily with the Montreal Canadiens. He plays baseball for the Lévis league.	The U.S.S.R. carries out its first atomic bomb tests.
Maurice Richard scores his 200th career goal.	Germany splits into the western-aligned Federal Republic and the Democratic Republic, part of the Soviet block.
Boxer Marcel Cerdan dies in an airplane crash. He has won 103 of his 107 fights.	Mao Tse-Tung proclaims the People's Republic of China.
	In South Africa, apartheid (racial segregation that deprives the majority black population of their basic rights) becomes official policy.
1950	**1950**
Bill Durnan, goalkeeper for the Canadiens, wins his sixth Vézina Trophy. At the close of the season, Durnan retires, giving up his place to Gerry McNeil.	Acting under the aegis of the UN, the United States moves into Korea after South Korea is attacked by communist North Korea.
Italian Nino Farina wins the first Grand Prix auto race.	
1951	
Michel, the Plantes' first son, is born.	
1952	**1952**
Jacques Plante replaces Gerry McNeil in the Habs' nets when the latter sustains a fractured	Elizabeth II is crowned Queen of Great Britain and Northern Ireland.

PLANTE AND THE WORLD OF SPORTS	CANADA AND THE WORLD

cheekbone. Jacques only lets in 4 goals in 3 games. Coach Dick Irvin Senior forbids his backup goalie to stand out from his teammates by wearing his lucky tuque during games.

Dwight Eisenhower is elected President of the United States.

French-language television is inaugurated in Quebec.

Elmer Lach of the Canadiens tops the NHL scoring standings.

Gold medallist Emil Zatopek of Czechoslovakia astonishes the world at the Helsinki Summer Olympics when he is the first runner to win all three track and field events at one Olympics.

1953
Jacques Plante plays his first playoff game with the Canadiens, against the Black Hawks in Chicago, winning with a 3-0 shutout. He also tends net in the game that eliminates Chicago in the semifinals.

1953
Nikita Khrushchev succeeds Joseph Stalin as General Secretary of the Soviet Communist Party.

The Korean War ends.

Jacques Plante's name is engraved on the Stanley Cup for the first time.

Jean Béliveau signs with the Montreal Canadiens.

1953-1954 season
When Jacques plays for the AHL Buffalo Bisons, the Canadiens' American farm-club, reporters dub him "Jake the Snake." He is called up to the Canadiens in February, plays 17 games, then is offered the position of number 1

1954
War in Indochina: France is forced to evacuate from its Vietnamese colony after a decisive communist victory at Diên Biên Phu. The Geneva Convention divides the country into North and South Vietnam.

goalie. He undergoes corrective surgery to his left wrist.

England's Roger Bannister runs a mile in less than four minutes.

1954-1955 season
Jacques Plante's first complete season in the NHL. His second son Richard is born.

Hockey fans riot in Montreal on St. Patrick's Day after Maurice Richard's suspension by NHL president, Clarence Campbell.

Marilyn Bell swims across Lake Ontario: 32 miles in 21 hours.

1955-1956 season
The "Flying Frenchmen" of the Canadiens, coached by Toe Blake, begin a five-year reign during which they consistently leave their adversaries in the dust. Jacques Plante wins his first Vézina Trophy and his first fully accredited Stanley Cup.

Jean Béliveau sets an NHL record for the highest number of goals scored by a centre.

Austrian Toni Sailer sweeps the gold medals in the men's downhill skiing at the Cortina Winter Olympics.

1956-1957 season
Jacques Plante suffers violent asthma attacks. He wins his second Vézina Trophy and his second

1955
The Warsaw Pact unites the Eastern bloc countries militarily.

1956
Egyptian President Nasser takes control of the Suez Canal, resulting in international hostilities; a UN force is sent to protect the canal and ease the British and French out of Egypt.

The popular rising in Hungary is savagely put down by Soviet troops.

Morocco and Tunisia become independent from France.

1957
John Diefenbaker of the Progressive Conservative Party is elected prime minister of Canada.

Jacques Plante

full-season Stanley Cup. In the summer, he wins the batting championship of the Quebec Senior Baseball League. He also writes a sports column for *La Voix*, a Shawinigan newspaper.

Argentinian Juan-Manuel Fangio wins his fifth title in Grand Prix automobile racing.

Mickey Mantle wins the American Baseball League (ABL) Triple Crown (best batting average, most home runs, and highest number of points in the season).

The European Economic Community is created, with a common parliament and economic policies.

The Sputnik satellite is successfully launched by the U.S.S.R.

Canadian diplomat and former minister of external affairs, Lester B. Pearson, wins the Nobel Peace Prize for his role in resolving the Suez Crisis.

In Montreal, five hundred people demonstrate against the naming of the Queen Elizabeth Hotel.

1957-1958 season
Jacques Plante wins his third consecutive Vézina Trophy and the Stanley Cup for the Habs. Bill Burchmore, of Fiberglas Canada and an ardent hockey fan, suggests moulding a protective mask to Jacques Plante's face.

Maurice Richard is the first NHL player to score 500 career goals.

Arnold Palmer wins the Masters Golf Tournament.

1958
The National Aeronautics and Space Administration (NASA) for space exploration is established in the United States.

General Charles De Gaulle is elected President of France.

1958-1959 season
Jacques Plante wins his fourth consecutive Vézina Trophy and the Stanley Cup. In the summer, he allows a face mould to be taken, and the first custom-made fibreglass goalie's mask is cast.

1959
In Quebec, Premier Maurice Duplessis dies in office.

The St. Lawrence Seaway is opened by Canada and the United States.

PLANTE AND THE WORLD OF SPORTS	CANADA AND THE WORLD

In the U.S., the American Football League (AFL) is created, giving competition to the NFL, established in 1920.

Fidel Castro leads a communist revolution in Cuba.

1959-1960 season
On November 1, Jacques Plante receives a serious facial injury in a game against the Rangers in New York. He returns to the ice wearing the mask for the first time in a regular game. Soon after, he becomes Burchmore's partner as exclusive manufacturer of the prototype goalie's mask. He wins his fifth consecutive Vézina Trophy, and the Canadiens win the Stanley Cup.

1960
In Quebec, Jean Lesage's Liberal Party gains power; the Quiet Revolution starts to transform Quebec society.

Amid gangster wars in Montreal, Mayor Jean Drapeau calls on Scotland Yard and the French police for help.

Democrat John F. Kennedy is elected president of the U.S.A.

Heavyweight boxer Cassius Clay wins the gold medal at the Summer Olympics in Rome.

The state of Louisiana is ordered by the U.S. government to integrate its public schools.

1960-1961 season
Plante, hampered by pain in his left knee, is sent down to the Montreal Royals of the Quebec Senior League. After a successful operation, he follows a rigorous training program during the summer. He also plays golf and renovates the family home in Laval-des-Rapides.

1961
The New Democratic Party of Canada (NDP) is founded, with Tommy Douglas as its leader.

The United States enters the Vietnam War.

Rocket Richard retires from professional hockey.

The East German government builds the Berlin Wall.

Bobby Hull of the Chicago Black Hawks demonstrates a slapshot that reaches a speed of 195 km. an hour.

Soviet astronaut Yuri Gagarin is the first human being to orbit the Earth.

Jacques Plante

PLANTE AND THE WORLD OF SPORTS	CANADA AND THE WORLD

In Squaw Valley, Ottawa skier Ann Heggtveit wins the Olympic gold medal in slalom; Canadian figure skaters Barbara and Paul Wagner win the gold medal for pairs.

1961-1962 season
Jacques Plante gives his best individual performance. He wins his sixth Vézina Trophy, and the Hart Trophy for most valuable player.

Jean Béliveau is named captain of the Montreal Canadiens.

In baseball, New York Yankee Roger Maris breaks Babe Ruth's 1927 record by hitting 61 home runs in a season.

Canadian figure skater Don Jackson wins the gold medal at the World Championships.

1962-1963 season
After a tough season, Jacques Plante is traded to the Rangers and moves to New York without his family. Lorne "Gump" Worsley takes over as the Habs' number 1 goaltender.

Jim Clark wins the world Grand Prix title for the first time.

Mickey Mantle hits a 183-metre home run for the Yankees.

1962
American astronaut John Glenn circles the earth in a spaceship.

The Cuban missile crisis brings heated tension to the Cold War. The U.S.S.R. backs down from using Cuba as a nuclear missile base, inaugurating the period of détente between the two world powers.

After a bitter struggle, Algeria becomes independent from France.

1963
Liberal "Mike" Pearson is elected prime minister of Canada.

John F. Kennedy, president of the United States, is assassinated in Dallas, Texas.

The separatist Rassemblement pour l'indépendence nationale (RIN) is established as a legitimate political party in Quebec.

Hydro-Québec is nationalized.

PLANTE AND THE WORLD OF SPORTS

1963-1964 season
Jacques Plante feels ill at ease in his new job; he suffers from homesickness. In summer, he plays for the Montreal Nationals in a newly revived lacrosse league. He writes weekly columns for the newspapers *Le Samedi* and *Le Nouveau Samedi*, and for the magazine, *Sports*.

At the Winter Olympics in Innsbruck, Austria, the Canadian bobsled team wins the gold medal for the first time.

1964-1965 season
Jacques Plante is sent down to the Baltimore Clippers of the American Hockey League. At the end of the season, he announces that he is leaving: his wife is ailing, and he will undergo surgery on his right knee.

Jean Béliveau is the first winner of the Conn Smythe Trophy, awarded to the most valuable player during the playoffs.

Sam Pollock becomes general manager of the Montreal Canadiens.

1965-1966 season
Jacques Plante starts his job as Molson Brewery representative. He plays lacrosse for the Caughnawaga Indians and participates in golf tournaments. He acts as television analyst during several

CANADA AND THE WORLD

1964
Under John Kennedy's successor, Lyndon Johnson, the American war in Vietnam escalates.

In the U.S.S.R., Nikita Khrushchev is stripped of his office and replaced by Leonid Brezhnev and Aleksei Kosygin.

1965
The maple leaf flag is adopted in Canada.

In the United States, black activist Martin Luther King leads the March for Equality in the fight against racial segregation.

1966
Daniel Johnson is elected Premier of Quebec for the Union Nationale Party.

The American Congress passes the Civil Rights Bill. Young Americans

Canadiens games. On December 15th, invited by Scotty Bowman, Jacques tends goal for the Junior Canadiens against the Russian National Team. He is named first star of the game, which the Russians lose 2-1.

Jim Brown of the Cleveland Browns sets a record for the highest number of career touchdowns in football.

Sandy Koufax, the great Los Angeles Dodgers pitcher, retires from baseball.

1967
The NHL expands into six Eastern Conference teams (the original NHL teams) and six new Western Conference teams (Philadelphia Flyers, Los Angeles Kings, St. Louis Blues, Minnesota North Stars, Pittsburgh Penguins, and Oakland Seals).

Plante helps coach Bert Olmstead with goalie training at the Oakland Seals' training camp.

Rogatien Vachon becomes Canadiens number 1 goaltender.

American Billie Jean King sweeps the major women's tennis titles.

Canadian skier Nancy Greene wins the World Cup.

protest against the war in Vietnam; the years of flower power, peace, and love begin.

In China, the Cultural Revolution is launched by Mao Tse-Tung.

1967
Expo '67: the Montreal World's Fair, during which Charles de Gaulle pronounces his famous *"Vive le Québec libre!"* speech.

The preliminary report of the Canadian Royal Commission on Bilingualism and Biculturalism recommends bilingualism in federal services.

The Six Day War in the Middle East ends when Israel bombs Cairo.

"The Colonels" suspend democracy in Greece in a military coup.

PLANTE AND THE WORLD OF SPORTS	CANADA AND THE WORLD

1968-69 season

Jacques Plante signs with the St. Louis Blues under coach Scotty Bowman, dividing goaltending duties with fellow veteran Glenn Hall. He wins his 7th Vézina Trophy, beating Canadien Bill Durnan's 1949 record.

Re-opening of the refurbished Montreal Forum, a transformation of the original 1924 building.

Don Drysdale of the L.A. Dodgers pitches six consecutive no-hit games.

Cassius Clay is stripped of his heavyweight title for refusing to fight in Vietnam.

Nancy Greene wins the gold medal in giant slalom and the silver in slalom at the Grenoble Winter Olympics.

1968

René Lévesque founds the Parti Québécois, proposing sovereignty-association with the rest of Canada.

Liberal Pierre Elliott Trudeau is elected prime minister of Canada.

Martin Luther King, apostle of nonviolence, is assassinated in Memphis. Robert Kennedy is also assassinated during the presidential primaries. Republican Richard Nixon is elected president.

In May, student protests shake De Gaulle's power in France.

In Czechoslovakia, the entry of Warsaw Pact tanks into Prague puts an end to Czech hopes of freedom from Soviet domination.

1969-1970 season

It is Jacques Plante's second season with the St. Louis Blues.

Bobby Orr of the Boston Bruins wins the scoring championship, the only defenceman to achieve this feat in NHL history.

The Montreal Expos begin to play at Jarry Park. Pitcher Claude Raymond is the first Canadian to play for the team.

1969

Conflict erupts in Quebec over Bill 63 on the use of French in the provincial education system.

Protests against the Vietnam War in the United States gather momentum.

Neil Armstrong is the first human being to walk on the moon.

Jacques Plante

PLANTE AND THE WORLD OF SPORTS	CANADA AND THE WORLD
	Yasser Arafat becomes head of the Palestinian Liberation Organization.
1970	**1970**
Jacques Plante is traded to the Toronto Maple Leafs. The Fibrosport company in Magog, of which Jacques Plante is 51-per-cent-owner, begins mass production of the hockey mask. Jacques' son Michel, twenty years old, takes over production operations.	In Quebec, the October Crisis occurs when the Front de Libération du Québec, a clandestine separatist group, kidnaps British diplomat James Cross and murders the provincial labour minister, Pierre Laporte. Prime Minister Trudeau implements the War Measures Act, temporarily suspending civil rights in Canada.
Plante meets Raymonde Udrisard, who will become his second wife.	Charles de Gaulle dies in France.
Two new teams join the NHL: the Vancouver Canucks and the Buffalo Sabres.	
Ken Dryden begins his nine-year reign as Canadiens goalie.	
1971	**1971**
The Jacques Plante Story, written by sportswriter Andy O'Brien in collaboration with Plante, is published.	Premier Robert Bourassa asks for Quebec's right to veto any changes to the Canadian constitution.
Guy Lafleur plays his first season as a right-winger for the Canadiens. Scotty Bowman debuts as Habs' coach.	
The World Hockey Association (WHA) is established to challenge the NHL.	

PLANTE AND THE WORLD OF SPORTS	CANADA AND THE WORLD

Evonne Goolagong, Australian Aboriginal tennis player, wins the French Open women's title.

1972

In July, Plante is invited by the Swedish Hockey Federation to teach goaltending techniques. His book, *Goaltending* is published in English and French. He works as a television analyst during the Canada-Russia hockey series.

The Atlanta Flames and the New York Islanders join the NHL.

Roberto Clemente, a Pittsburgh Pirate with over 3000 base hits to his credit, dies in an accident.

Russian gymnast Olga Korbut is the marvel of the Munich Summer Olympics.

1973

Plante is traded to the Boston Bruins late in the season. He negotiates a ten-year million-dollar contract as coach-manager of the Quebec Nordiques of the WHA. He writes a weekly column for the daily, *À-propos.*

Baseball great Willie Mays retires after twenty-two seasons.

1972

The Watergate break-in scandal erupts during the U.S. election campaign.

Eleven Israeli athletes are kidnapped and murdered by Palestinian terrorists at the Munich Olympics.

1973

The Americans withdraw from Vietnam and Saigon falls to the communist forces of Ho Chi Minh.

The Yom Kippur War in the Middle East leads to a rise in oil prices.

In Chile, a violent military coup overthrows the elected socialist government of Salvador Allende.

In Canada, the LeDain Commission recommends the legalization of marijuana.

Jacques Plante

1974-1975 season

In May, Plante resigns as Nordiques coach. He plays his last season, at forty-five years of age, as goaltender for the WHA Edmonton Oilers. He moves to Sierre, Switzerland, his home for the remaining years of his life.

Guy Lafleur scores over 50 goals in his season with the Canadiens.

The greatest batter of all time, Hank Aaron of the Atlanta Braves, hits his 715th career home run, eclipsing Babe Ruth's record.

Jimmy Connors, Bjorn Borg, and Chris Evert dominate world tennis tournaments.

1975

After the death of his younger son, Richard, Jacques Plante retires from play. For the next eleven years, he will work as adviser and goaltending trainer for several teams, including the Philadelphia Flyers, the Montreal Canadiens, and the St. Louis Blues.

The Canadiens play their first international game, against the Red Army Hockey Team.

American golfer Jack Nicklaus wins the Masters Tournament for the fifth time.

Tennis ace Arthur Ashe is the first Afro-American to win at Wimbledon.

1974

Bill 22 proclaims French the official language of Quebec.

U.S. President Nixon is forced to resign because of his role in the Watergate coverup.

Civil government is restored in Greece after seven years of military dictatorship.

1975

In Spain, parliamentary monarchy is restored after the death of General Franco.

In Vietnam, the southern army capitulates to the communist forces of the north; the country is unified a few months later.

In Cambodia, the Maoist Khmer Rouge takes power.

In Lebanon, civil war rages between Muslims and Phalangists.

PLANTE AND THE WORLD OF SPORTS	CANADA AND THE WORLD

1976

Jacques Plante is the TV analyst during the Canada Cup series.

The Summer Olympics are held in Montreal. Romanian Nadia Comaneci, age fourteen, shines in gymnastics, winning three gold medals with seven perfect scores.

1976

René Lévesque's Parti Québécois wins the Quebec provincial election.

In the United States, Jimmy Carter becomes president.

1978

Jacques Plante is inducted to the Hockey Hall of Fame.

Molson Brewery purchases the Montreal Canadiens Hockey Club.

Formula One driver Gilles Villeneuve of Berthierville, Quebec, wins the first Montreal Grand Prix.

Martina Navratilova dominates women's tennis (and will continue to do so until the mid-80s).

1978

The Italian Christian Democrat leader, Aldo Moro, is assassinated by the Red Brigades in Rome.

John Paul II is elected Pope.

1982

Gilles Villeneuve is killed in a collision during the pre-race trial runs for the Belgian Grand Prix.

1985

Plante is chosen as goalie of the Montreal Canadiens dream team.

Pete Rose of the Cincinnati Reds beats Ty Cobb's 1928 record for the most base hits in a career.

1985

Mikhail Gorbachev becomes head of the Soviet Communist Party. His meeting with American president Ronald Reagan leads to an easing of Soviet relations with the West.

PLANTE AND THE WORLD OF SPORTS	CANADA AND THE WORLD

1986

Jacques Plante dies of stomach cancer on February 27th, in Geneva. He is buried in Sierre.

The Montreal Canadiens win their 23rd Stanley Cup, and the Habs' young goaltender, Patrick Roy, wins the Conn Smythe Trophy.

1994

Jacques Plante is inducted into the Quebec Sports Pantheon.

1995

The Montreal Canadiens club retires the number 1 (Jacques Plante's number) from its uniforms.

1986

In the Philippines, President Marcos is deposed and replaced by Corazón Aquino.

The world's most serious nuclear power station accident occurs at Chernobyl in the Ukraine.

Sources Consulted

This book is based on articles and columns in various newspapers and magazines, some of which no longer exist, and others of which are still going strong: *The Gazette*, *La Presse*, *Le Journal de Montréal*, *Le Journal de Québec*, *Le Soleil*, *Montréal-Matin*, *La Patrie*, *Le Petit Journal*, *Parlons sport*, *Hockey Québec*, *Sports*, *La Revue des Canadiens*, *Maclean's*, *Nouvelles illustrées*, etc.

Two books, one written and the other co-written by Jacques Plante were also valuable sources:

PLANTE, Jacques, *Goaltending*, Collier-Macmillan of Canada, 1972.

O'BRIEN, Andy, with Jacques Plante, *The Jacques Plante Story*, McGraw-Hill Ryerson, 1972.

Other books consulted were:

BEAUCHAMP, Jacques, *Le sport c'est ma vie*, Éditions Québecor, Montreal, 1979.

BRODEUR, Denis, *30 ans de photographie*, Éditions de l'homme, Montreal, 1993.

HOLLANDER, Zander, and Hal BOCK, *The Complete Encyclopedia of Hockey*, New American Library, New York, 1983.

HUNTER, Douglas, *A Breed Apart: An Illustrated History of Goaltending*, Viking, New York, 1995.

IRVIN, Dick, *The Habs, An Oral History of the Montreal Canadiens 1940-1980.*

Index

Printed in June 2001
at AGMV/Marquis,
Cap-Saint-Ignace (Québec).